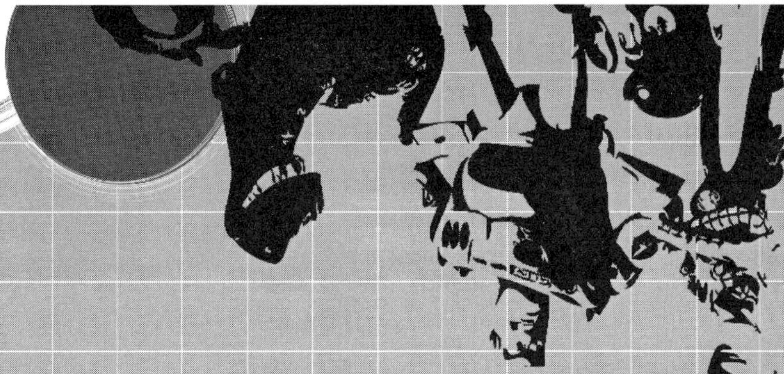

SCREEN ENGLISH

Toy Story 3

The Simpsons

Shrek

The Emperor's New Groove

이봉형 지음

신아사

SCREEN ENGLISH

Contents

일러두기 ······ 5

1. Toy Story3 ······ 7

Plot ······ 9
Preview ······ 10
Dialogue ······ 12
Music Break - Musical Cats: Memory ······ 16
Review ······ 18
Activity 1-1 ······ 19
Dialogue ······ 21
Review ······ 30
Activity 1-2 ······ 32

2. The Simpsons ······ 35

Plot ······ 36
Preview ······ 38
Dialogue ······ 40
Music Break - Solveig's Song ······ 46
Review ······ 47
Activity 2-1 ······ 48
Dialogue ······ 50
Review ······ 54
Activity 2-2 ······ 55
Music Break - The Beatles: Let it Be ······ 57

3. Shrek ······ 59

Plot ······ 60
Preview ······ 62
Dialogue ······ 64

Review ··· 68
Activity 3-1 ··· 69
Dialogue ··· 71
Review ··· 76
Music Break - Simon & Garfunckle: Bridge Over Troubled Water ··· 77
Activity 3-2 ··· 80
Dialogue ··· 82
Review ··· 84
Activity 3-3 ··· 85
Dialogue ··· 87
Review ··· 92
Activity 3-4 ··· 94
Music Break - Movie Avatar: I See You ··· 96

4. The Emperor's New Groove ··· 99

Plot ··· 100
Preview ··· 102
Dialogue ··· 104
Music Break - You Raise Me Up ··· 108
Review ··· 109
Activity 4-1 ··· 110
Dialogue ··· 112
Review ··· 115
Activity 4-2 ··· 116
Dialogue ··· 118
Review ··· 121
Actvity 4-3 ··· 122
Dialogue ··· 124
Review ··· 130
Activity 4-4 ··· 132
Music Break - Movie Titanic: My Heart Will Go On ··· 134

Worksheet: Taking Dictation Practice in Lyrics ··· 137

일러두기

국내 어느 대학이든 영화를 비롯한 영상물을 활용한 영어강좌가 빠짐없이 개설되어 있다. 강좌명이 Screen English 이든 "영상영어"라고 하든 상관없이 영상물을 이용하면 영어학습에 특별한 효과가 있을 것이라는 기대감 때문일 것이리라. 저자도 최근 몇 년간 영상물을 활용한 강좌를 교양강좌로 개설하여 강의를 해오고 있다.

해마다 달라지는 학생들의 영어학습에 대한 기대감에 부응하고자 명작영화, 명연설문, 다큐멘토리, 여행자를 위한 특정 도시 홍보물, YouTube clip 등 나름대로 다양한 내용을 가지고 강좌를 운영한 결과 내용면에서 영화가 가장 흥미유발의 효과가 있음을 깨닫게 되었다.

본 교재는 4편의 애니메이션 영화 Toy Story 3, The Simpsons, Shrek, The Emperor's New Groove를 교재로 구성한 것이다. 애니메이션 영화는 청소년뿐 만 아니라 성인들이 보아도 내용면에서 손색이 없으며 영어학습에 집중해야 하는 영어강좌에서 내용이나 영어표현의 면에서 학습용으로 최적이라는 판단이 든다. 문어체가 아닌 구어체 영어를 접할 수 있는 절호의 기회이기도 하다.

대학생들은 피땀 흘려 이제껏 쌓아온 자신의 영어지식을 밖으로 끄집어 내어 표현하는 연습이 절실하다. 물론 제2언어 학습자로서 현재 가지고 있는 영어지식이 완벽할 수는 없다. 중요한 것은 자신의 영어지식을 말로 그리고 글로 써보는 시간을 많이 가질 필요가 있다는 것이다. 더구나 우리 학생들이 영어로 말할 때 보면 대화체가 아닌 문어체에 가까운 영어를 구사한다. 글을 쓸 때도 지나치게 bookish한 어휘들을 쓰느라 고생한다. 언어는 문어체 보다는 구어체가 바탕이 되어야 한다. 글을 통한 의사소통 보다는 말을 통한 의사소통의 기회가 훨씬 많기 때문이다.

미국의 TV에 등장하는 사람치고 말을 더듬거리는 사람이 별로 없다. 평소 준비된 답변을 하는 것도 아닌데 말이다. 그것은 초등학교 때부터 말하기 훈련을 해 왔기 때문이다. 말재간이 동양인들 보다 뛰어나기 때문은 아닐 것이다. 다른 이유는 말을 중시하는 서양사회의 분위기도 한몫 한다고 볼 수 있다. 조용조용 얘기하기 보다는 또렷하게 자신감 넘치는 말투로 의사표현을 하는 습성이 몸에 배어 있다. 유교적 전통이 남아있는 우리 사회의 말에 대한 관념과는 차이가 있다.

영화 속의 영어는 영어권 사람들이 일상 생활에서 매일같이 사용하는 구어체 표현들이다. 그 중에는 점잖지 못한 속어들도 없지 않아 있지만 상당수는 일반적인 대화에서 무리 없이 사용할 수 있는 표현들이다. 우리가 익혀야만 비로소 영어다운 영어로 의사소통이 가능한 것들이다. 본 교재의 역점이 바로 여기에 있다.

영화의 대본을 보기 전에 Background와 Plot을 먼저 배치한 이유는 전체 내용에 대해 미리 감을 잡은 후 영어에 집중하여 훈련을 하기 위한 것이다. 다음으로 Preview난에 영화 속에 등장하는 일상적인 표현 등 영어의 진수임에도 우리 입에서 쉽게 나오지 않은 표현들을 맛보게 하였다. 아마 여기 나오는 표현 중 상당부분은 학습자들이 이미 알고 있을 것이다. 영어학습이 여기에 그쳐서는 곤란하다. 영어현장에서 이러한 표현을 말 그리고 글로 사용할 수 있어야 한다.

영화 중간이나 말미에 Review난을 둔 이유는 반복학습을 위한 것이다. 또한 적지 않은 표현들이 시나리오 작가들이 의도한 것도 아닌데 4편의 영화에 약속이나 한듯이 반복해서 나타나고 있다. 그만큼 자주 쓰이는 표현들이란 의미이다. 이미 알고 있는데 영어공부에 무슨 도움이 되느냐고 반문할 수 있다. 반복의 횟수가 많을수록 이 표현들을 자신의 것으로 만드는데 도움이 된다는 점을 명심할 필요가 있다. 이해가 아닌 체득을 하여야만 실제 상황에서 이러한 표현들이 용수철처럼 튀어 나올 수 있다. 수동적 언어행위에 해당하는 읽기와 듣기로 만족할 것이 아니라 말하기와 쓰기와 같은 능동적 언어행위를 수행하는 것이 우리의 목표이기 때문이다.

강의진행 중 영화의 일정 장면을 놓고 학생들을 소그룹으로 나누어 연기를 해보게 하는 것도 매우 효과적일 것이다. 학생들이 잠시 배우가 되어 남 앞에서 말해보기 (speak up)를 해보는 것만큼 효과적인 경우는 드물기 때문이다. 자신이 완전히 의미를 이해하고 연습을 해 본 표현만이 실전에서 사용 가능하다고 장담할 수 있다. 하나를 제대로 아는 것이 여럿을 어설프게 아는 것 보다 훨씬 나으리라.

각 영화에 2회에서 4회까지의 연습문제가 제시되어 있다. 과제로 부과하여 영어표현 익히기, 영어로 자신의 생각 표현하는 훈련을 하기 위한 것이다. 속담 익히기는 주옥 같은 이러한 표현들을 입에 익히면 영어로 말문을 트는데 매우 도움이 될 것으로 판단하기 때문에 매 연습문제 마다 4개씩 제시하였다. 적어도 이들 표현만큼은 언제 어디서든지 무의식 중에 사용가능할 정도로 익히기를 기대한다.

본문에서 다룬 7개 노랫말 받아쓰기 훈련을 위해 책의 말미에 Dictation worksheet을 추가하였다. 학생들의 수업 집중력을 끌어 올리는데 도움이 될 것으로 보인다.

아무쪼록 교재를 이용하는 모든 학습자들에게 구어체 영어 습득에 도움이 되어 영어 의사소통에 큰 발전이 있기를 기대한다. 마지막으로 출판을 허락해 주신 신아사 한규갑 상무님, 류선희 선생께 감사 드린다.

2012년 여름
저자 이봉형 씀

1. Toy Story 3

2010년도 Pixar Animation에서 제작하고 Walt Disney Pictures에서 영화 분배를 맡는 영화로 상영시간은 103분이다. 1995년 출시된 이래 3탄까지 나올 정도로 애니메이션 영화 역사상 box-office 흥행수입 기준 가장 성공을 거둔 작품이다. Pixar Animation은 Steve Jobs가 Apple사를 본의 아니게 떠나 있던 기간에 CEO로 일했던 애니메이션 전문 영화 촬영소이다. 2006년 Walt Disney Pictures에 인수합병 되었다.

Plot

18살이 된 Andy가 대학에 진학하여 집을 떠나게 되면서 그 동안 같이 지내온 장난감들은 자신들이 버림받지 않을까 전전긍긍한다. Andy는 Woody만 가져가고 Buzz를 비롯한 나머지 장난감은 다락방에 올려다 놓겠다고 작정한다. 그러나 Andy 엄마는 Andy가 장난감들을 담아놓은 쓰레기 봉지를 버리는 것으로 잘못 알고 쓰레기차가 수거해 가도록 도로변에 내다 놓는다. Woody만이 이 사실을 인지하고 장난감들에게 주인의 실수로 이렇게 되었으니 기지를 발휘하여 Andy네 집으로 돌아가자고 설득하나 장난감들은 믿지 않는다. 이들은 Sunnyside라는 Day Care로 갈 것을 고집한다. 이들의 소원대로 Sunnyside에 도착하니 Lotso라는 이름을 가진 곰인형이 친절하게 맞이해 준다. 이들은 안도의 한숨을 내쉬나 그것도 잠시뿐. 이들이 함께 놀아줄 아이들은 장난감들을 마구 부수고 던지는 난폭한 아이들이었고 사실은 Dare Care의 장난감 왕초 노릇을 하는 Lotso는 전형적인 폭군으로 순진한 장난감들을 이용하고 있다는 사실을 뒤늦게 깨닫고 후회한다. Woody의 말이 거짓이 아니었음도 깨닫는다.

그러나 이미 이들은 Lotso의 마수에 걸려들어 탈출이 어려운 수용소 생활을 연상케 하는 신세로 유일한 탈출구는 쓰레기차라는 말을 듣는다. 그리고 Lostso의 옛 동료 장난감 Chuckle로부터 Lotso가 극악무도한 폭군이 된 내력을 듣는다. 드디어 철통 같은 경계망을 뚫고 이들은 탈출을 감행한다. 이들을 체포하려는 Lotso 일당의 추격도 시작된다. 탈출 도중 가련한 신세가 된 장난감들은 쓰레기 처리장에 내동댕이쳐 지면서 갖은 수난과 삶과 죽음의 갈림길을 수 차례 겪은 후 구사일생으로 생명을 부지한다. 이들 장난감들은 지긋지긋한 수용소 같은 Dare Care 탈출에 성공하자마자 자신들을 보호해 줄 것으로 믿는 Andy가 아직 학교로 출발하지 않았음을 확인하고 Andy네 다락방으로 직행한다. Woody의 지략으로 Andy는 Woody를 포함하여 자신의 모든 장난감을 Bonnie라는 장난감을 극진히 아끼는 아이에게 맡기고 홀가분한 마음으로 길을 떠난다. 장난감들이 새 주인을 만나 안도하며 Woody에게 손을 흔들며 아쉬운 작별을 고한다. 會子定離의 진리의 여운을 남기면서 이 영화는 끝을 맺는다.

❊ Preview

Don't miss our **one shot** sale!

단 한번의 세일기회를 놓치지 마세요!

It's **a long shot** for the player to win the title.

그 선수가 타이틀을 차지할 가능성은 희박하다.

My puffy totally **messed with my stuff**.

강아지가 내 물건들을 엉망으로 만들어 놓았다.

Turning 30, her skill is **over the hill**.

30이 되면서 그의 기량이 하향곡선을 그리고 있다.

Please let me **off the hook** this time.

이번만은 봐주세요.

Let's set a date for **spring cleaning**.

대청소 날짜를 잡자.

Do you **need a hand** with your homework?

숙제 도와 주련?

What's the point of studying math? I have never used a sine and cosine in my daily life.

수학공부가 무슨 소용이람? 살아가면서 사인이나 코사인을 써먹은 적이 없는 걸.

They completely **lost their marble** at the shocking news.

그 사람들은 충격적인 소식에 완전히 제정신이 아니었다.

It is time that we did more to protect the weak and poor.

약자와 가난한 사람들을 보호하기 더 일할 때다.

Get it through your vinyl noggin (=head).

꼼량 껏 이해해 봐.

Her athletic career **was washed up** by the time she was 25.

25이 되면서 그 여자는 운동선수로서는 한 물 갔다.

Remember to **keep** things in **perspective**.
사태 전체를 보는 안목을 갖는 것을 잊지 말라.

Susan, I **haven't seen you in ages**.
수잔 정말 오랜만이야.

You have been through a lot today.
오늘 고생들 많았습니다.

I'll be back in **a jiff**.
곧 돌아 오겠습니다.

Everybody concerned that his ideology **is far out.**
모두들 그 사람의 이념이 극단으로 치달아 걱정이다.

Wake up at this critical moment.
이 중요한 순간 정신 차려라.

He seems to **belong** to the people there well.
그는 거기 사람들하고 잘 어울리는 것 같다.

Unhand me at once. I'm innocent.
이 손 놓으세요. 저는 죄가 없습니다.

Let go of me!
저 놓아 주세요.

The pediatrician arrived **in the nick of time**
그 소아과의사가 마침 잘 도착했다.

During the war they **ran low** on every supply.
전쟁 중 모든 보급품들이 떨어져 갔다.

Haste often **neutralizes** our efforts.
이따금 성급해서 애쓴 보람이 없게 된다.

You scared the hell **out of me**.
정신이 나갈 정도로 무서웠다.

His busy schedule disallowed him to **make it** to the conference.
그 사람은 바빠서 학회에 오지 못했다.

You'd better to **chew on** what you said.
네가 말한 바를 되새겨 보는 것이 좋을 거야.

Dialogue

1. Young Andy Goes Wild with Toys

YOUNG ANDY Buzz! Shoot your laser at my badge! Woody, no! It'll kill you! Just do it! You're going to jail, Bart. Mom...!

ANDY'S MOM No, no...! Keep playing! Just pretend I'm not here.

ANDY No, it's okay, Mom! It's... a 50-foot baby from outer space! She's **on a rampage**! Run for your lives!

MOM Does the red light mean it's going? Come on, say Happy Birthday' to Molly...

YOUNG ANDY (mouth full) Happhy Birthday!

MOM Oh, charming.

YOUNG ANDY Happhy Birthday!!!

MOM Look how tall you're getting!

ANDY Buzz Lightyear to the rescue! Good work, Buzz!

(Music: Our friendship will never die)

2. Operation Playtime

WOODY Okay — places, everyone! C'mon. C'mon. Get in position!

MRS. POTATO HEAD Wait — I can't find my other eye!

HAMM Someone's foot is in my face...

MR. POTATO HEAD It's mine! Give it back!

ALIENS You saved our lives! We are eternally grateful!

JESSIE Buzz, mind if I squeeze in next to ya?

BUZZ Yes! No! I mean...! Why would I mind?! Squeezing next to you! Is it hot in here?

REX Here they come!

WOODY Sarge! You got it...!

SARGE Mission accomplished!

WOODY Careful...! Careful!!! All right, guys. We got **one shot** at this. Everyone ready?

JESSIE We're ready, Woody! Let's do it!

WOODY Buzz — make the call.

BUZZ Target is on approach.

WOODY Just like we rehearsed it, guys...

ANDY Hello...? Hello...? Anyone there?

Molly, stay outta my room!

MOLLY I wasn't in your room!

ANDY Then, who was **messing with my stuff**?

MOLLY It wasn't me...!

MR. POTATO HEAD Well, that went well!

REX He held me! He actually held me!

HAMM Oh, this is just sad.

MR. POTATO HEAD Who are we kiddin'? The kid's seventeen years old!

WOODY Guys, hey, hold up! We need a staff meeting! Everyone? A staff meeting!

HAMM Not again...!

WOODY Oh, come on! Slink? Gather everyone up!

SLINKY Uh... We are gathered, Woody!

WOODY Okay. First off — we all knew Operation Playtime was **a long shot**..

MR. POTATO HEAD More like a misfire!

WOODY But we've always said this job isn't about getting played with. It's about...

JESSIE Being there for Andy. We know.

3. Andy Goes to College

REX But we can try again, right?

WOODY I'm callin' it, guys. We're **closin' up shop**. Andy's going to college any day now. That was our last shot.

BUZZ We're going into Attic Mode, folks. Keep your accessories with you at all times — spare parts, batteries... Anything you need for an orderly transition.

MR. POTATO HEAD "Orderly?" Don't you get it?! We're done! Finished! **Over the hill**!

WOODY Hey, hey, now come on, guys! We all knew this day was coming!

HAMM Yeah, but now it's here!

WOODY Look, every toy goes through this! No one wants to see their kid leave!

BUZZ Hey! Sarge! What are you doing?

SARGE War's over, folks. Me n the boys are movin' on.

……

SOLDIER ONE And let's face it — when the trash bags come out, we Army guys are the first to go.

BUZZ Trash bags...?!

WOODY Who said anything about trash bags?

SARGE It has been an honor serving with you. Good luck, folks.

WOODY No, no... Wait...! Wait! Wait!!!

REX We're getting thrown away?

WOODY No! No one's getting thrown away!

MR. POTATO HEAD How do you know?!

JESSIE We're being abandoned...!

BUZZ We'll be fine, Jessie!

……

WOODY Whoa, whoa! Hold on! Quiet!!! No one's getting thrown out, okay?! We're all still here, aren't we?! I mean, yeah, we've lost friends along the way — Wheezy and Etch and...

REX Bo Peep...?

WOODY Even... Even Bo. All good toys who've gone on to new owners. But through every **yard sale**[1], every **spring cleaning**, Andy held on to us. He must care about us, or we wouldn't be here. You wait —Andy's gonna tuck us in the attic. It'll be safe and warm...

BUZZ And we'll all be together.

4. Junk or Soul Mate?

MOM Okay, Andy, let's get to work here. Anything you're not taking to college either goes in the attic, or it's trash.

ANDY Mom, I'm not leaving 'til Friday!

MOM C'mon — it's garbage day.
Look, it's simple: Skateboard? College. Little league trophy? Probably's attic. Apple core? Trash. You can do the rest.

MOLLY Why do you still have these toys?

ANDY Molly, out of my room...!

MOLLY Three more days and it's mine...!

---

[1]*yard sale*: garage sale. a sale for used stuff, mostly when someone moves out.

MOM Molly, you're not **off the hook** either! You have more toys than, you know, what to do with. Some of 'em could make other kids really happy...

MOLLY What kids...?

MOM The children at the day care. They're always asking for donations.

MOLLY But, Mom...

MOM No "buts". You choose the toys you wanna donate. I'll drop 'em off at Sunnyside.

……

ANDY Mom — no one's gonna want those old toys. They're junk!

MOM Fine. You have 'til Friday — anything that's not packed for college, or in the attic, is getting thrown out.

ANDY Whatever you say, Mom.

……

ANDY You **need a hand**?

MOLLY I got it...

ANDY Here. So, you gonna miss me when I'm gone?

MOLLY If I say 'no', do I still get your room?

ANDY Nope.

MOLLY Then, yes, I'll miss you.

……

WOODY That's not trash! That's not trash!!
Think, Woody...! Think! Think!
Buster! C'mere, boy! C'mere! Okay, boy! To the **curb**[2]! Hyah!!! No, Buster, no...!

JESSIE We're on the curb!

MR. POTATO HEAD Oh, I knew it would come to this!

BUZZ Pull, everyone! Pull!!!

REX It won't rip!

HAMM Ah, forget it! It's triple-ply high density polyethylene!

BUZZ There's gotta be a way out!

MR. POTATO HEAD Andy doesn't want us! **What's the point**?

BUZZ Push! Push!!!

REX I can hear the garbage truck! It's getting closer-fffmmm!

---

[2]*curb*: a rim or edge of stones or concrete along a street or a roadway.

Music Break

Musical Cats : Memory

Midnight,
not a sound from the pavement.
Has the moon lost her memory?
She is smiling alone.
In the lamplight, the withered
leaves collect at my feet,
and the wind begins to moan.

Memory,
All alone in the moonlight,
I can dream of the old days.
Life was beautiful then.
I remember the time
I knew what happiness was.
Let the memory live again.

Every street lamp seems to beat
a fatalistic warning.
Someone mutters,
and the street lamp gutters
and soon it will be morning.

Daylight,
I must wait for the sunrise,
I must think of a new life
and I musn't give in.
When the dawn comes,
tonight will be a memory too
and a new day will begin.

Burnt out ends of smoky days,
the stale cold smell of morning.
The street lamp dies,
another night is over,
another day is dawning.

Touch me,
it's so easy to leave me,
all alone with my memory
of my days in the sun.
If you touch me,
you'll understand
what happiness is.
Look, a new day has begun

❊ Review

Hooligans **went on a rampage** after the soccer match.
훌리건들이 축구경기 후 난동을 부렸다.

Don't miss our **one shot** sale!
단 한번의 세일을 놓치지 마세요.

It's **a long shot** for the player to win the title.
그 타이틀을 차지할 가망은 희박하다.

My puffy totally **messed with my stuff**.
강아지가 내 물건들을 엉망으로 만들어 놓았다.

The strikers **closed up shop**.
농성자들은 판은 접었다.

Turning 30, her skill is **over the hill**.
그녀의 기량은 30을 넘기면서 하향곡선을 그렸다.

Please let me **off the hook** this time.
이번 만은 봐 주세요.

Let's set a date for **spring cleaning**.
대청소 날짜를 잡읍시다.

Do you **need a hand** with your homework?
숙제 좀 도와주련?

What's the point of studying math? I have never used a sine and cosine in my daily life.
수학공부가 무슨 소용이 있나? 살아가면서 사인과 코사인을 써먹은 적이 없다.

❊ Activity 1-1

I. Try it on in English.

1. 뒤늦게 후회한들 무슨 소용이 있나?

2. 누구도 봐주지 않는 것이 우리의 방침이다.

3. 단 한번의 기회를 놓치지 말라.

4. 이번 골프대회에서 그 사람이 우승할 가능성은 높지 않다.

5. 누가 내 머리를 엉망으로 만들어 놓았나?

6. 중앙로에서 술취한 사람이 난동을 부리고 있다.

7. 그 야구선수의 기량은 예전만 못하다.

II. Answer the given questions and develop your idea.

1. What do you think of Woody, a leading character among the toys in this movie?

2. Toys are destined to move on to a day care center. It is believed that the used items are actually donated to various organizations and individuals in the United Sates. What are your ideas on the culture to recycle used items to be used by others, instead of throwing away as garbage?

III. Words We Live By

1. A house is not a home.

2. A person is known by the company he keeps.

3. A problem shared is a problem halved.

4. Absolute power corrupts absolutely.

Dialogue

5. Heading to Sunnyside, a Day Care

WOODY What's going on? Don't you know this box is being donated!

BUZZ It's under control! We have a plan!

REX We're going to Day Care!

WOODY Day Care?! What — have you all **lost your marbles**?!

MRS. POTATO HEAD Didn't you see? Andy threw us away!

WOODY No...! No, no, no! He was putting you in the attic!

MRS. POTATO HEAD Attic? So how'd we end up on the curb?!

WOODY That was a mistake! Andy's Mom thought you were trash!

HAMM Yeah! After he put us in a trash bag!

MRS. POTATO HEAD And called us "junk"!

WOODY I know it looks bad but, guys, ya gotta believe me!

MR. POTATO HEAD Sure thing, "College Boy"!

JESSIE Andy's movin' on, Woody! **It's time we did the same**.

WOODY Okay, out of the box! Everyone, right now! Come on! Buzz — gimme a hand. We gotta get this thing outta here!

BUZZ Woody — wait! We need to figure out what's best for every — ...

……

WOODY Okay, everyone, **listen up**... We can get back to Andy's, but we gotta move fast. We'll hide under the seats 'til we get home...

MRS. POTATO HEAD **Get it through your vinyl noggin**[3], Woody — Andy doesn't want us anymore!

WOODY He was putting you... in the attic!!!

JESSIE He left us... On the curb!

BUZZ Alright, calm down! Both of you!

WOODY Okay, fine! Just wait'll you see what Day Care's like!

REX Why...? What's it like?

WOODY Day Care is a sad, lonely place for **washed-up** old toys who have no owners.

---

[3]*noggin*: wooden brick to be filled, instead of regular bricks, for the purpose of driving nails at the spot.

HAMM Quite the charmer, aren't ya?

WOODY Oh, you'll see! As soon as we get to Day Care, you'll be begging to go home.

6. At Sunnyside

WOODY Okay, calm down, guys. Let's **keep this in perspective**...

MR. POTATO HEAD Perspective?! This place is perfect!

REX Woody, it's nice! See, the door has a rainbow on it!

MOM Hey, there!

RECEPTIONIST Wow! **Haven't seen you in ages**...

MOM Just wanted to drop these old toys off. Is this Bonnie?! Look how big you are!

RECEPTIONIST Say hi, sweetie!

BONNIE Hi.

RECEPTIONIST How are your kids? Molly and Andy?

MOM Not kids anymore. Andy's going to college on Friday. Can you believe?

RECEPTIONIST You sure they won't miss these?

……

LOTSO Well, hello there! I thought I heard new voices! Welcome to Sunnyside, folks! I'm Lots-o'-Huggin' Bear! But, please, call me Lotso!

BUZZ Buzz Lightyear. We come in pea....

LOTSO First thing you gotta know about me... I'm a hugger!! Oh, look at y'all! **You been through a lot today, haven't you**?

MRS. POTATO HEAD Oh, **it's been horrible**!

LOTSO Well, you're safe now. We're all cast-offs here — we been dumped, donated, yard-saled, second-handed, and just plain thrown out. But just you wait — you'll find being donated was the best thing that ever happened to ya!

REX Mr. Lotso...? Do toys here get played with every day?

LOTSO All day long. Five days a week.

JESSIE But what happens when the kids grow up?

LOTSO Well, now, I'll tell ya — when the kids get old, new ones come in. When they get old, new ones replace them. You'll never be outgrown or neglected. Never abandoned or forgotten. No owners means no heartbreak.

……

KEN	**Far out**! Hey, hi, everybody!
	Down **in a jiff**, Lotso! So, Who's ready for Ken's Dream Tour?
LOTSO	Let's show our new friends where they'll be stayin'!
KEN	Folks, if you wanna step right this —

……

LOTSO	Well, thank you, Big Baby. Why don't you come meet our new friends? We were thrown out together, me him. Abandoned by the same owner!

……

JESSIE	Woody — **wake up**! It's over! Andy is all grown up! .
WOODY	Okay, fine! Perfect! I can't believe how selfish you all are. So this is it? After all **we've been through**?

……

BONNIE'S MOM	Bonnie!
Bonnie	Coming!

7. Heading out of Sunnyside

LOTSO	Ken...! What's going on here?! Why's this toy tied up?
KEN	He... He got out, Lotso!
LOTSO	Got out? Oh, no, no, no! This isn't how we treat our guests! There you go. I'm so sorry.
BUZZ	Lotso, there's been a mistake.
LOTSO	A mistake...!!!
BUZZ	The children in the Caterpillar Room are not age-appropriate for me and my friends. We respectfully request a transfer to the Butterfly Room.
LOTSO	Well, request granted!
KEN	But, Lotso...
LOTSO	Hush now, Kenneth! This Toy's shown initiative! Leadership! Why, I'd say we found ourselves a keeper! (to others) Hear that, everyone?! We got a keeper! World Champion! This gang, we're callin' you up to the **Big Leagues**[4], son! From now on, you'll have anything you want!
BUZZ	Excellent! I'll **go get** my friends.
LOTSO	Whoa, whoa! Hold on there, Boss! Those Caterpillar kids need someone to play with...!

---

[4]*Big League*: Like major league baseball, a group of top level teams.

BUZZ But **my friends don't belong there**!

LOTSO Oh, none of us do! I agree! Which is why — for the good of our community we ask the newer toys, the stronger ones, to take on the hardships the rest of us can't bear anymore.

……

BUZZ What are you...? What?! **Unhand me**!

LOTSO Bring in The Bookworm.

……

BUZZ What are you doing?! **Let go of me**!

LOTSO (reading) "To return your Buzz Lightyear Action Figure to its original factory settings, slide the switch from PLAY to DEMO..."

……

MRS. POTATO HEAD Okay, Wait, Mom. Why is he so upset? Oh, no! Oh, this is terrible!

……

LOTSO How're y'all doin' this fine evening?

JESSIE Oh, thank heavens! Have you seen Buzz?

MRS. POTATO HEAD There's been a mistake! We have to go!

LOTSO Go?! Why, you just got here! **In the nick of time**, too! We were **runnin' low on** volunteers for the little ones! They just love new toys, now don't they?

MRS. POTATO HEAD Love?! We've been chewed! Kicked! **Drooled on**[5]! Just look at my **pocketbook**[6]!

LOTSO Well, here's the thing, Sweet Potato — you ain't leavin' Sunnyside.

MRS. POTATO HEAD Sweet Potato?! Who do you think you're talking to? I have over thirty accessories and I deserve more respec —

……

LOTSO Lightyear! Explain our overnight accommodations.

BUZZ Yes, sir! Prisoners sleep in their cells! Any Prisoner caught outside their cell spends the night in The Box! ···Any prisoner misses **roll call**[7] spends the night in The Box! ··· Prisoners do not speak unless spoken to! Any prisoner talks back spends the night...

LOTSO **At ease***, soldier! They're **neutralized**! But remember. They'll say anything to make you doubt yourself!

---

[5] *drool on*: run at the mouth.

[6] *pocketbook*: purse.

[7] *roll call*: calling of a list of names as of soldiers or students.

BUZZ Don't worry, Commander! Any doubt I had **got pounded out of me** at the Academy!

……

MR. PRICKLEPANTS Sunnyside is a place of ruin and despair, ruled by an evil bear who smells of strawberries!

WOODY Lotso...?

BUTTERCUP He may seem plush and huggable on the outside. But inside, he's a monster!

WOODY But... How do you know that?

MR. PRICKLEPANTS He'll tell you!

CHUCKLES Yeah, I knew Lotso. He was a good toy. A friend. Me and him, we had the same kid — Daisy... I was there when Lotso got unwrapped. She hugs him — love at first sight. Daisy loved us all, but Lotso... Lotso was special. They did everything together. You never seen a kid and a toy more in love. One day, we took a drive...A sleeping Daisy is carried to the car. After lunch, Daisy fell asleep. ...Lotso wouldn't give up. It took forever, but we finally **made it** back to Daisy's. But by then, it was too late. His universe is shattered. Something changed that day inside Lotso. Something **snapped**...

LOTSO She replaced us. C'mon!

BIG BABY No, she only replaced yo —!

8. Nightly Roll.Call

KEN Tyrannosaurus... Rex

REX Here

KEN Barbie...

BARBIE Here...

KEN Potato Head

Potato Head...Potato Head?

BUZZ Hey! **Tuberous**[8] Root Man! Wake up! Impossible! Hey!

KEN Little late for a stroll, eh, Potato Head?

MR. POTATO HEAD That's Mr. Potato Head to you, Smoothie!

KEN You're turning out to be quite the trouble-maker, aren't ya? What'd you

[8] *tuberous*: (Botnay) a rounded thickening of a subterranean stem as the potato.

think you were gonna do? Whatz right outta here?

9. Fixing Buzz.

WOODY So how do we fix Buzz?

……

BUZZ Help! Prison riot!

HAMM Give it up. No one can hear you.

……

WOODY Quick, open his back! There's a switch!

BUZZ Unhand me, Zurg scum! The Galactic courts will show you no mercy!

WOODY It's not working! Why's it not working? Where's the manual?

HAMM Here we go! There should be a little hole under the Switch!

WOODY Little hole. Got it!

HAMM (reading) To reset your Buzz Lightyear, insert paper clip....

WOODY Rex, use your finger!

……

HAMM All right, let's see... "Caution: Do not hold button for more than five seconds."

REX It's not my fault!

SPANISH BUZZ Bitácora Espacial — Me he despertado de hipersueño en un planeta extraño. (I've awakened from hypersleep on a strange planet)

10. Truth Be Told

LOTSO (incredulous) What are you doin'?! Runnin' back to your kid? He don' want you no more!

WOODY That's a lie!

LOTSO Is it? Tell me this, Sheriff — if your kid loves you so much, why is he leavin'? Y'think you're special, Cowboy? You're a piece of plastic! You were made to be thrown away! Speak of the devil...! Now we need toys in our Caterpillar Room. And you need to avoid that truck. Why don't you come on back, join our family again?

JESSIE This isn't a family, it's a prison! You're a liar and **a bully**[9] and I'd rather not in this dumpster than join any family of yours!

---

[9] *bully*: a person who are used to threat and harass smaller or weak people

BARBIE	Jessie's right! Authority should derive from the consent of the governed! Not from the threat of force!

……

LOTSO	I didn't throw you away. Your kid did. Ain't one kid ever loved a toy, really! **Chew on** that when you 're at the dump! .
WOODY	Wait...! What about Daisy?
LOTSO	I don't know what you're talking about.
WOODY	Daisy...? You used to do everything with her!
LOTSO	Yeah — then she threw us out! She replaced us!
WOODY	She replaced you! And if you couldn't have her, no one could! You lied to Big Baby and you been lying ever since!
LOTSO	Where'd you get that...?!
WOODY	She loved you, Lotso...
LOTSO	She never loved me!
WOODY	As much as any kid ever loved a toy!

11. In the Garbage Truck: Almost Doomed

JESSIE	Buzz, you okay?! Buzz! Buzz!!! No...!
BUZZ	That wasn't me, was it?
JESSIE	Oh, Buzz! You're back!!! You're back, you're back, you're back!!!
BUZZ	Yes, I'm back! Where've I been?
WOODY	Beyond Infinity, Space Ranger!
BUZZ	Woody! But... Where are we now?!
REX	(excitable) In a garbage truck on the way to the dump!
WOODY	Everyone — stay together! Hold on! We're going in...!
MR. POTATO HEAD	You got all your pieces?
ALIEN	The Cla-a-a-aw!

……

LOTSO	Help...! Help me!!! I'm stuck! Help!!! Please!
Woody	Lets go.
JESSIE	Woody...!

12. Farewell to Andy.

MOM	Honey, you want some food for the road?

ANDY	I'll get something on the way.
BUZZ	You know where to find us, Cowboy.
MOM	Did you say goodbye to Molly?
ANDY	Mom, we've said goodbye like ten times!
MOM	Oh, Andy...!
ANDY	Mom...! It's okay...
MOM	I know, it's just... I wish I could always be with you.
ANDY	You will be, Mom.
MOLLY	Hey... Aren't you gonna say goodbye to Buster?
ANDY	Of course I will...! Who's a good doggie?! Who's a good doggie?!!! I'm gonna miss you!
MOLLY	He's telling you to go already. C'mon, get the rest of your things.

......

ANDY	Hey, Mom... So, you really think I should donate these?
MOM	It's up to you, honey. Whatever you want to do.

......

ANDY	Hi!
BONNIE'S MOM	Wow! Look at you! I hear you're off to college?
ANDY	Yeah. Right now, actually.
BONNIE'S MOM	So, what can we do for you?
ANDY	Uhh... I have some toys here.
BONNIE'S MOM	Ohhh...! You hear that, Bonnie?
ANDY	So you're Bonnie? I'm Andy. Someone told me you're really good with toys. These are mine, but I'm going away now, so need really special to play with them. This is Jessie — the roughest, toughest cowgirl in the whole West. She loves **critters**[10], but none more'n her best pal, Bullseye. Yee-haw! Here. This is Rex the meanest, most terrifying dinosaur who ever lived. "Raaawwwrrrrr...!!!" The Potato Heads — Mister and Missus. You gotta keep 'em together, cause they're madly in love. Slinky here is as loyal as any dog you could want. But Hamm? He'll keep your money safe ......but he's also one of the most **dastardly**[11] villains of all time...

......

ANDY	Now, Woody — he's been my pal as long as I can remember. He's brave, like a cowboy should be. And kind, and smart. But the thing that makes

---

[10] *critters*: animals and plants

[11] *dastardky*: cowardly, meanly base

Woody special? Is he'll never give up on you — ever. He'll be there for you, no matter what. Y'think you can take care of him for me? (she nods) Okay, then.

……

WOODY So long, partner.

❊ Review

The accident is **under control**.

사태가 수습되고 있다.

They completely **lost their marble** at the shocking news.

그 사람들은 충격적인 소식에 완전히 넋을 잃었다.

It is time that we did more to protect the weak and poor.

약자와 빈민들을 보호하기 위해 더 일 할 때이다.

Get it through your vinyl noggin (=head).

네 잘난 머리로 이해해 봐!

Her athletic career **was washed up** by the time she was 25.

그 여자는 25이 되면서 운동선수로는 한 물 갔다.

Remember to **keep** things **in perspective**.

사태 전체를 볼 줄 알아야 한다.

Susan, I **haven't seen you in ages**.

정말 오랜만이야 수잔.

You **have been through a lot today**.

오늘 고생들 많았습니다.

I'll be back **in a jiff**.

곧 올께요.

Everybody concerned that his ideology **is far out.**

그 사람이 이면이 극단으로 흘러 걱정이다.

Wake up at this critical moment.

이 중요한 순간에 정신 차려야지.

We've been through.

우린 끝났어.

He seems to **belong** to the people there well.

거기 사람들과 잘 어울려.

Unhand me at once. I'm innocent.

이 손 놓으세요. 저는 죄가 없습니다.

Let go of me!

저 놓아 주세요.

The pediatrician arrived in **the nick of time.**

소아과 의사가 마친 때맞춰 도착했다.

During the war they **ran low on** every supply.

전재중 모든 보급품이 떨어져 갔다.

Haste often **neutralizes** our efforts.

성급한 나머지 흔히 허사가 되고 만다.

You scared **the hell out of me**.

넋이 나갈 정도로 무서웠다.

His busy schedule disallowed him to **make it** to the conference.

그 사람 바빠서 학회에 맞춰서 오기가 힘들었다.

The storm **snapped** the oak tree into two.

폭풍우로 오크나무가 두 동강이 났다.

You'd better to **chew on** what you said.

말한 바를 곱씹어 보렴.

❊ Activity 1-2

I. Try it on in English.

1. 적의 박격포 공격을 무력화시켜야 한다.

2. 방망이를 부러뜨리는 일은 그에게는 어렵지 않다.

3. 그 사람이 나에게 말한 말을 곱씹어 보았다.

4. 오늘 고생들 많이 하셨습니다.

5. 그 축구선수는 한물갔다.

6. 화재가 수습되고 있다.

7. 오랜만 입니다.

8. 이 손 놓으세요.

9. 그 여자는 새 친구들과 잘 어울리고 있다.

10. 이러한 경쟁의 시대에 정신 차려야 한다.

11. 전체를 볼 줄 알아야 한다.

12. 너 마침 잘 왔다.

13. 그 사람 보내 주세요.

II. Answer the given questions and develop your idea.

1. Toy Story series have been acclaimed as deserving every moviegoers' love as was done to another preeminent animation, *Snow White* in the1930s. What do think about the craze for animation?

2. At first, Andy wanted to take only Woody when he moves on to college. Yet, he changed his mind to take them all to Bonnie, a toddler nice to toys. What do you think of the conclusion of this movie?

III. Words We Live By

1. Beauty is in the eye of the beholder.

2. Every stick has two ends.

3. He who laughs last laughs longest.

4. If life deals you lemons, make lemonade.

2. The Simpsons

1989년부터 방영되기 시작한 TV series로서 미국 TV에서 *Jeopardy*, *Larry King Live* 등과 함께 20년 이상 long-run 하는 프로그램 중의 하나이다. 장르는 애니메이션 sitcom이다. 시청자들의 호응이 좋아 이를 2007년도에 영화화한 것이 영화 The Simpsons이다. 물론 시나리오는 새롭게 쓴 것이다. 등장인물은 TV series에 등장하는 Homer의 가족인 Homer, Marge, Bart, Lisa, Maggie와 Grampa, Colin, Milhouse, Cargill, Ralph, Nelson 등 이들의 주변 인물들이다. 미국의 그리 넉넉지 못한 working class에 속하는 평범한 사람들의 삶과 현대사회의 커다란 사회적 문제인 환경문제를 결부시켜 재치있는 코믹 터치를 가미하여 보는 이로 하여금 실소를 자아내고 cartharsis의 기회를 제공해 준다. 본래 Homer의 직장이 원자력발전소라는 점에서 환경문제가 영화 소재로 채택된 것으로 보인다. 가공의 도시이면서 친숙한 이름을 가진 Springfield가 작품의 배경이다.

Plot

영화는 Springfield 호수에서의 록밴드 공연으로 시작한다. 공연자 한 사람이 환경문제 토론을 제안하자 관중들이 거세게 항의한다. 그 사이 밴드단원이 서 있던 바지선 (barge)이 오염된 호숫물에 녹아내리고 결국 단원들이 익사하고 만다. 교회 추도예배에서 할아버지가 닥쳐올 도시의 운명을 예언하는 듯한 언행을 보이지만 아무도 주목하지 않은 가운데 Marge만이 관심을 보인다.

家長 Homer는 엉뚱하게 돼지를 집안에 데려와 반려동물 삼아 지극정성을 다한다. 문제는 돼지의 분비물을 버리지 않고 통에 쌓아둔 것이다. Marge의 성화에 못이겨 쓰레기처리장에 가서 처리하려는 순간 공짜 도넛을 준다는 전화를 받고 황급히 인분 통을 호수에 버리고 도망친다. 호수는 심하게 오염되어 한 번 들어갔다 나온 다람쥐에 돌연변이가 발생한다. 이 환경오염은 당국 (EPA)에 알려져 터미네이터 Schwarzenegger 대통령에게 보고된다. 환경국장 Cargill은 5개의 해결안 중 하나를 대통령에게 선택하도록 하는데 대통령은 무심코 이 도시를 대형 유리 돔으로 덮는 안을 택하고 이 도시를 지도에서 삭제해 버린다. 한편 호수오염의 주범이 Homer라는 사실이 알려지면서 동네사람들이 Homer를 죽이려 들이닥치지만 그와 가족들은 sinkhole을 통해 돔 밖으로 용케 빠져 나오는 행운을 누린다. 무일푼인 이들 가족은 오토바이곡예로 차를 손에 넣고 알래스카로 도주해 새로운 인생을 시작한다.

돔에 갇힌 시민들은 돔을 탈출하기 위해 무진 애를 쓰지만 불발로 끝난다. 당국에서는 분노하고 거의 jitters 지경에 이른 시민들의 봉기가 두려워 국정운영이 세심하지 못한 터미네이터 Schwarzenegger 대통령을 부추겨 아예 이 도시를 폭파해 버리는 음모를 꾸민다. 이 소식을 알게 된 Marge, Homer, Lisa 일행은 Springfield로 달려가 옛 고향사람들을 구하려 하지만 Homer는 주저한다. 자신을 죽이겠다고 달려든 고향 사람들에 대한 악몽이 남아 있었기 때문이다. 홀로 남은 Homer는 결국 인디언 여인주술사의 도움으로 곰의 공격을 모면하고 이 여인의 계시 (epiphany)를 받아 고향으로 달려간다. 막상 천신만고 끝에 고향에 도착해 보니 돔을 폭파하기 위해 환경당국 헬기가 돔 정중앙 구멍을 통해 시한폭탄을 로프에 매달아 드리우는 장면을 목격한다. Homer는 돔 꼭대기까지 기어올라가 로프를 타고 내려가 폭탄을 끌어 올리려다 그만 폭탄도 땅에 떨어뜨리고 로프를 타고 탈출하려던 사람들도 로프에서 떨어지는 참사가 발생한다. 또 다시 Springfield의 천덕꾸러기가 되어 죄책감에 빠져있던 Homer는 어찌할 바를 모르던 중 자신의 장기인 오토바이 타기를 생각하게 된다. 폭탄을 든 Bart를 태우고 오토바이 곡예를 부리며 폭발까지 2분도 채 남지 않은 시한폭탄을 돔의 정중앙 구멍을 향해 힘껏 내던진다. 돔의 끝자락에 걸려 폭발한 폭탄은 인명피해 없이 돔을 산산조각 내어 사람들을 해방시킨다. 마침내 Homer를 증오하던 사람들도 그를 받아들이고 Homer도 과거의 불명예를 극복하게 된다. 이제 Springfield 주민들은 오랜만에 구사일생으로 일상으로 복귀한다.

❇ Preview

If you ask me, the quality is not good.
구태여 말하자면 품질이 좋지 않습니다.

They **touched on** a vital issue.
중요한 문제를 건드렸다.

I **beg to differ**.
제 의견은 다릅니다.

She envies her sister **like hell**.
자기 언니를 엄청 부러워한다.

Well-said.
말 잘했다.

Piece of cake.
누워서 떡 먹기야.

The story of the farmer's success is a pure **myth**.
그 농부의 성공은 지어낸 이야기야.

He **canvassed** the neighborhood from house to house for order.
그는 가가호호 방문하며 주문을 받았다.

He **took the rap** for his boss.
상사를 대신해서 벌을 받았다.

He is **out of control**.
그 사람은 통제가 안돼.

It's at my wits' end.
어쩔 수 없었습니다.

What's the catch?

조건이 뭐죠?

I'm **off the hook.**

그래 봐도 자유로운 몸이야.

The machine **is stuck.**

기계가 꼼짝달싹하지 않는다.

Am I **getting through** to you?

제 목소리 들리세요?

Don't be **a drama queen**.

오버하지 마세요.

It's **the time of year** when azalea blossoms there.

매년 이 맘 때면 진달래가 핀다.

Please **bear with me** until I finish my story.

제 말 끝날 때까지 기다려주세요.

Three bottles of beer are **on the house.**

맥주 3병 써비스로 드립니다.

Keep a low profile.

자세를 낮추세요.

I'**m much obliged** for your help.

도와주셔서 무척 감사합니다.

Risk your life to save our country.

나라를 구하기 위해 생명을 무릅쓰다.

Dialogue

1. In the Theatre

CAT	We come in peace for cats and mice everywhere.
MOUSE	Hey, how you doing? Good to see you. Thanks for coming out.
	……
HOMER	Boring.
LISA	We can't see the movie.
HOMER	I can't believe we're paying to see something we get on TV for free. **If you ask me**, everybody in this theatre is a giant sucker. Especially, you.

2. Green Day Concert

A FAT MAN	Excuse me. My heinie is dipping.
A SINGER	All right. Well, thanks a lot for coming. We've been playing for three and a half hours. Now, we'd like just a minute of your time to say something about the environment.
AUDIENCE	You suck! Shut up and play. Preachy!
A BANDMAN	We're not being preachy. But the pollution in your lake, it's dissolving our barge.
LISA	I thought they **touched on a vital issue**.
A MAN	**I beg to differ.**
	……
PASTOR	For the latest rock band to die in our town…Lord, hear our prayer.
AUDIENCE	Lord, hear our prayer.
MARGE	I hate being late.
HOMER	I hate going. Why can't I worship the Lord in my own way…by praying **like hell** on my deathbed?
MARGE	They can hear you inside.
HOMER	Relax! Those pious morons are too busy talking to their phony-baloney God. How you doing? Peace be with you! Praise Jebus.
	……

PASTOR	Today I'd like to try something a little different. I'm going to call on one of you! Now, the word of God dwells within everyone. I want to let the word out. Let your spirit···

3. Homer's Chores

HOMER	Take out hornets' nest. Check "Fix sinkhole." Check "Re-shingle roof." Steady. Steady··· Why, you little···! I'll teach you to laugh at something that's funny.
BART	You know, we are on the roof. We could have some fun.
HOMER	What kind of fun?
BART	How about a dare contest?
HOMER	That sound fun. I dare you to··· climb the TV antenna!
BART	**Piece of cake**.
HOMER	Earthquake! Aftershock!
FLANDERS	Homer, I don't mean to be a **Nervous Pervis**[12]··· but if he falls, couldn't that make your boy a **paraplege-arino**[13]?
HOMER	Shut up, Flanders.
BART	Yeah, shut up, Flanders.
HOMER	**Well-said**, boy.

4. Lisa's Canvass

LISA	Hello, sorry to bother you on a Sunday but I'm sure you're as worried about the pollution in Lake Springfield as I am. Lake Springfield has higher levels of mercury than ev —
A NEIGBOR	Why, it's the little girl who save my cat.
LISA	Lake Springfield···
MILHOUSE	Come on over, Lisa. You can **canvass** me as long as you want.
LISA	Milhouse, you don't care about the environment.
MILHOUSE	Hey, I am very passionate about the planet.
A BAD GUY	Say global warming is **a myth**.
MILHOUSE	It's a myth! Further study is needed!
A BAD GUY	That's for selling out your beliefs.

---

[12] *(Pervis Ellison)* A former NBA player.

[13] paraplegia + ino ('little, Italian suffix)

5. Kids' Stuff

A voice (of unknown boy) Are you aware that a leaky faucet can waste over⋯.?

LISA	Two thousand gallons a year.
BOY	Turning off lights can save⋯
LISA	Enough energy to power Pittsburg.
BOY	And if we kept our thermostats at 68 in winter⋯.
LISA	We'd be free from our dependency of foreign oil in 17 years.
BOY	I'm Colin.
LISA	I haven't seen you at school.
COLIN	Just moved from Ireland. My dad's a musician⋯.

6. The Ultimate Dare

HOMER	What seems to be a problem, officers?
BART	Tell him you dared me to do it.
OFFICER	If that's true, then you should be **taking the rap** here, not your son.
HOMER	And what happens to me if it's my fault?
OFFICER	You'll have to attend a one-hour parenting class.
HOMER	It was all his idea! He's **out of control**, I tell you! It's **at my wits' end**.
OFFICER	See you in court, kid.

7. Spider Pig

CAMERAMAN	Action!
CLOWN	Hey, Hey. It's your old pal Krusty for my new pork sandwich, the Klogger. If you can find a greasier sandwich, you're in Mexico! And, we' re clear, perfect, cut, print, kill the pig!
	⋯⋯
HOMER	What? You can't kill him if he's a wearing people clothes! You're coming home with me.
HOMER	You nailed her. He also does me. You smiled. **I'm off the hook**. Oh! You have so many looks.
BART	So that's what snug is.
	⋯⋯
HOMER	I have a nibble.

8. An Irritating Truth

LISA We are at the tipping point, people. If we don't do something now···
I'm sorry I lost my train of thought. Isn't he dreamy?

MAYOR Agreed.

LISA Okay, so here's **the bottom line**. If we don't change our ways right now. Pollution in Lake Springfield will be at the level.

A MAN That's not so bad. No, the lift is stuck. **Am I getting through to** anyone?

AUDIENCE Hell, yeah. We need a new one of those things.

MAYOR All in favor of new scissor lift. Say "aye"

LISA No! This lake is just one piece of trash away from a toxic nightmare. But I knew you wouldn't listen.

9. Dumping Crap into the Lake

MARGE What's going on here?

HOMER Nothing, Nothing. I'm not sure that pig should be in the house. And by the way, what are you doing with his leavings?

HOMER Don't worry. I devised a most elegant solution.

MARGE It's leaking.

HOMER It's not leaking. It's overflowing.

MARGE He filled up the whole silo in just two days.

HOMER Well, I helped.

MARGE Homer! Stop! Stop. I know it's easy for your mind to wander but I want you to really concentrate on me.

······

A MAN Homer, you gotta get over here. Health inspector shut down the doughnut store. They're giving out free doughnuts!

HOMER Oh, my God, my God! I just got one thing I gotta do first.

A MAN Well, you'd better hurry. They're going fast.

10. Elected to Lead, Not to Read

HEAD OF EPA Pollution in Springfield has reached crisis levels.

PRESIDENT I hate this job. Everything is "crisis" this and "end of the world" that.

	Nobody opens with a joke. I miss Danny DeVito.
HEAD	You want a joke, huh! Stop me if you've heard this one.
PRESIDENT	Look at those angry eyes and giant teeth. It's like Christmas at the Kennedy Compound.
HEAD	You know, sir, why you made me head of the EPA. You appointed one of the most successful men in America··· to the least successful agency in government. And why did I take the job?
	......
PRESIDENT	I was elected to lead, not to read. Number three.

11. Stuck in a Dome

A BOY	We're being sealed in a dome!
A MAN	What do I do? I don't know what to do! If I stay, I'm trapped. If I leave, I'm alone. Oh, God, In. Out. In. Out! I never saw Venice.
	......
POLICE OFFICER	Open fire! Who's hurt? Raise your hands.Without the attitude.
MAN	People, people. I have an important announcement. I have just perfected an acid-firing super-drill, which can cut through anything.
ANOTHER MAN	Hey, that's cool.
CARGILL	Environmental Protection Agency.
AUDIENCE	Come again! **A drama queen**.

12. Trappuccino

NEWSMAN	The dome has put an end to life as we know it. The town is running low on supplies of everything from gasoline to Botox. Moment, please. Now, as always, we end our news on "The Lighter Side." **It's the time of year** when the swallows return to Springfield.
	......
NEWSMAN	A shocking discovery has been made here at Lake Springfield.
HOMER	That could be anybody's pig crap silo.
MARGE	Homer, it was you. You single-handedly killed this town.
HOMER	I know it's weird.

NEWSMAN Just a reminder, this station does not endorse **vigilante justice**[14], unless it gets results. Which it will.

[14] *vigilante justice*: legal actions by unofficial organization.

Music Break

Solveig's Song

The winter may pass and the spring disappear
The spring disappear
The summer too will vanish and then the year
And then the year

But this I know for certain: you'll come back again
You'll come back again
And even as I promised you'll find me waiting then
You'll find me waiting then

Oh-oh-oh ....

God help you when wand'ring your way all alone
Your way all alone
God grant to you his strength as you'll kneel at his throne
As you'll kneel at his throne

If you are in heaven now waiting for me
In heaven for me
And we shall meet again love and never parted be
And never parted be!

Oh-oh-oh ....

❊ Review

I'm **off the hook**.

나는 자유의 몸이야.

They **touched on** a vital issue.

중요한 문제를 그들이 건드렸어.

I **beg to differ.**

제 생각은 좀 다른데요.

She envies her sister **like hell**.

그녀는 자기 언니를 엄청 부러워한다.

Well-said.

말 잘했다.

Piece of cake.

누워서 떡 먹기.

The story of the farmer's success is a pure **myth**.

농부 성공담은 지어낸 이야기야.

He **canvassed** the neighborhood from house to house for order.

주문을 받기 위해 가가호호 방문했다.

He **took the rap** for his boss.

상사 벌을 대신 받았다.

He is out of control.

그 사람 통제가 안돼.

It's at my wits' end.

저도 어쩔 수 없었습니다.

Don't **be a drama queen**!

오버하지 마세요.

It's the time of year when azalea blossoms there.

매년 이 맘 때면 진달래가 핀다.

❊ Activity 2-1

I.Try it on in English.

1. 동의할 수 없습니다.

2. 말 잘 했다.

3. 누워서 떡 먹기야.

4. 매년 이 맘 때면 날씨가 춥다.

5. 컴퓨터가 먹통이 됐다.

6. 사람들은 불이 나자 어찌할 바를 몰랐다.

7. 물가가 통제불능상태가 되었다.

II. Answer the given questions and develop your idea.

1. What's the general attitude of men living at Springfield about environment?

2. What measures did the government take for the solution of pollution of Lake Springfield?

III. Words to Live by

1. Better safe than sorry.

2. Better late than never.

3. If wishes were horses, beggars would ride.

4. It's the squeaky wheel that gets grease.

Dialogue

13. Screw Up and Back up

CARGILL I want roving death squads around the perimeter 24/7. I want 10,000 tough guys, and I want 10,000 soft guys…..

HOMER I've always been afraid I'd screw up our lives so badly. We'd need a backup plan. And that plan is right here! No, nope, bingo. **Bear with me**. Alaska, a place where you can't be too fat or too drunk, where no one says things like: "Let's see your high-school equivalent certificate."

MARGE I don't know, Homie.

HOMER I'm not saying it right. Look, the thing is, I can't start a new life alone. And I've really come to like you guys.

MARGE I just don't see it.

……

BART How are we supposed to get to Alaska without any money?

HOMER All right, son. If you don't believe in me, believe in America. America,where anymen can make quick money with no questions asked.

……

A MAN (in an amusement park) Step right up and win my truck! All you have to do is conquer the Ball of Death.

HOMER **What's the catch**?

OWNER No catch. Just ride the motorcycle all the way around just one time. Three times for $10.

HOMER Marge, how much money do we have?

……

OWNER That's two. That's three. Here what I'll do because I like seeing you hurt yourself. I'll give you one **on the house**.

HOMER You're the best.

14.Welcome to Alaska

NEWSMAN Day 37 under the dome. We are facing intermittent power failures which ….

BAR OWNER Okay, very funny. I'm gonna turn the lights off again. When they come back on, I want all my booze back, the way it was.

……

HOMER What? This isn't the way I pictured Alaska at all......

……

SECURITY Welcome to Alaska. Here, thousand dollars.

HOMER Well, it's about time. But why?

SECURITY We pay every resident $1,000 to allow oil companies to ravage our state's natural beauty.

HOMER I'm home.

15. Knowing Things is Overrated

NEWSMAN Day 93 under the dome. With necessities growing dangerously low… Who knows what spark will set off the powder keg?

……

CARGILL You know what that is, sir?

PRESIDENT A crack?

CARGILL Exactly.

CARGILL People got out of the dome before. They're gonna get out again, When they do, there's gonna be hearings, investigations….

PRESIDENT I'll have to go back to make family comedies.

CARGILL Don't worry. I have a solution for you, sir. In fact, I have five solutions. You don't have to read them. You'll have deniability. I'll take care of it. You know nothing.

PRESIDENT No, I need to know what I'm approving.

CARGILL Absolutely. But on the other hand, knowing things is overrated.

16. On the Train to Springfield without Homer

BART Did you see that?

MARGE Yes, they're going to destroy Springfield. But we're going to stop them. Homie, get your clothes on, Homie?

HOMER I'm happy here. Screw Springfield!

……

MARGE I can't believe you'd say something so selfish…….

MARGE	Get down from there. We have to **keep a low profile**···till we get to Seattle to tell the world of the plot to destroy Springfield.
LISA	I don't know if you guys should be talking so loud.
MARGE	Oh, Lisa, it's not like the government is listening to everybody's conversations

17. Homer, Left Alone in Alaska

OLD WOMAN	Do you know why you are here?
HOMER	Because my family cares more about other people than they do about me.
OLD WOMAN	Drink this liquid.
HOMER	More, please.
OLD WOMAN	Now we'll cleanse your spirit by the ancient Inuit art of throat singing.
HOMER	Throat singing? How long are we doing this?
OLD WOMAN	Until you have an **epiphany**[15].
HOMER	Okay.

……

OLD WOMAN	Don't give up, Homer. You're closer than you think.
HOMER	But which way do I go? **Much obliged**.

18. Under the Escort

AGENT	Look, we can't keep stopping at every "sop""yeld" or "one vay" sign. Just move on.
BART	Let us out! Let us out!
AGENT	Stop that. You'll scratch your shackles.
BART	I hope I do.
LISA	Oh, way to go, Bart.
BART	You, stink.

---

[15] *epiphany*: sudden realization

19. Tricked by an Idiot

CARGILL Attention, Springfiled. Your government has realized that putting you inside this dome was a terrible mistake. Therefore, we're commencing with Operation Soaring EAGLE.

……

MAN Hey, if one of us distracts Cargill, the rest of us can climb up that thing.

……

CARGILL I was tricked by the idiot.

IDIOT Hey, I know how you feel. I was beat in **tic-tac-toe**[16] by a chicken.

20. Homer at Springfield

HOMER Hey, I tried my best. What am I supposed to do? But how am I supposed to get up there? Here, buy yourself something nice.

GRAMP Homer, what the hell are you doing now?

HOMER **Risking my life** to save people I hate… for reasons I don't understand. Gotta go!

21. Homer Came Back

BART Now, that was a great father-son activity.

CARGILL Hello, Homer.

HOMER So we meet at last, whoever you are!

HEAD There're a couple of things they don't teach you at Harvard Business School. One is how to cope with defeat and how to handle a shotgun. I'm going to do both right now.

BART Wait! If you kill my dad...you'll never know where the treasure is buried.

……

MARGE Best kiss of my life.

HOMER Best kiss of your life so far.

---

[16]*Tic-tac-toe*: a pencil-and-paper game for two players, X and O, who take turns marking the spaces in a 3×3 grid. The X player usually goes first. The player who succeeds in placing three respective marks in a horizontal, vertical, or diagonal row wins the game. Who won in the following?

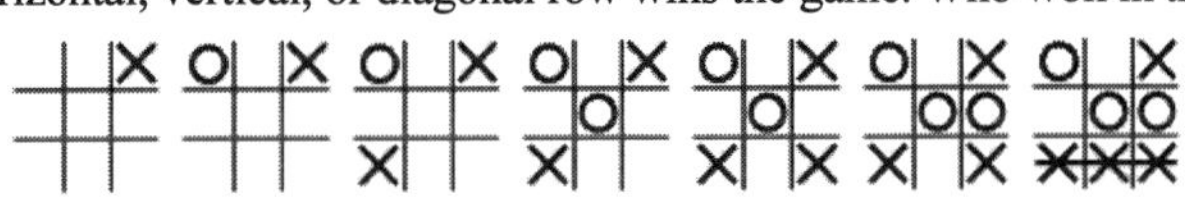

❊ Review

Please **bear with me** until I finish my story.
내 말씀 끝날 때까지 잠깐만요.

Three bottles of beer are **on the house**.
맥주 3병 서비스입니다.

Keep a low profile; Keep a high profile.
자세를 낮춰야지. 앞에 나서거라.

I'm much obliged for your help.
도와주셔서 대단히 감사합니다.

Risk your life to save our country.
국가를 구하기 위해 생명을 무릅쓰다.

What's the catch?
조건이 뭐죠?

❊ Activity 2-2

I.Try it on in English.

1. 태워주셔서 감사합니다.

2. 음료수는 써비스로 드립니다.

3. 눈에 띄지 않게 해라.

4. 제 얘기를 끝까지 들어 주세요.

5. 나는 군에서 총 다루는 법을 배웠다.

6. 계백장군은 목숨 바쳐 백제를 구하기 위해 싸웠다.

7. 네가 일을 망쳤구나!

II. Answer the given questions and develop your idea.

1. Can you describe the government's second scheme about the polluted Springfield?

2. Ultimately, Homer and his family happily reunited at Springfield. How did Homer come to his home safe, and recover from his former fault?

III. Words to Live by

1. The sun shines on all alike.

2. Opportunity makes the thief.

3. It takes all sorts to make a world.

4. Never judge a book by its cover.

Music Break

The Beatles : Let It Be

When I find myself in times of trouble
Mother Mary comes to me
Speaking words of wisdom
Let it be
And in my hour of darkness
She is standing right in front of me
Speaking words of wisdom
Let it be

Let it be, let it be
Let it be, let it be
Whisper words of wisdom
Let it be

And when the broken hearted people
Living in the world agree
There will be an answer
Let it be
For though they may be parted there is
Still a chance that they will see
There will be an answer
Let it be

Let it be, let it be
Let it be, let it be
there will be an answer

Let it be
Let it be, let it be
Let it be, let it be
Whisper words of wisdom
Let it be

Let it be, let it be
Let it be, let it be
Whisper words of wisdom
Let it be

And when the night is cloudy
There is still a light that shines on me
Shine until tomorrow
Let it be
I wake up to the sound of music
Mother Mary comes to me
Speaking words of wisdom
Let it be

Let it be, let it be
Let it be, let it be
There will be an answer
Let it be
Let it be, let it be
Let it be, let it be
Whisper words of wisdom
Let it be

3. Shrek

2001년 컴퓨터 애니메이션 코메디 영화. 원작은 William Steig 동화 Shrek! 이 영화의 성공으로 제작사 Dream Works사는 1995년 Toy Story를 제작한 Pixar사와 에니메이션 분야에서 경쟁자 반열에 오르게 된다. Shrek은 이 회사의 마스코트가 되어 Shrek2, Shrek the Third, Shrek Forever After, Shrek the Halls, Scared Shrekless가 후속 편으로 나온다.

Plot

늪에서 평화롭게 살아가던 괴물 Shrek은 어느 날 Farquaad 악당에 의해 살던 곳에서 쫓겨난 동화 속의 귀찮은 요정들의 침입을 받고 당황해 한다. Shrek은 Farquaad에게 자신의 늪을 돌려줄 것을 요구하기로 한다. 당나귀가 동행한다. 한편 Farquaad는 동화 속의 조무래기들 행방을 놓고 Gingerbread Man을 닦달한다. 그 때 호위병 중 하나가 Magic Mirror를 가져온다. 거울은 말하기를 Farquaad는 공주와 결혼해야만 왕이 될 수 있다고 한다. 거울은 그에게 세 명의 공주 Cinderella, Snow White, Fiona의 모습을 보여준다. Farquaad는 거울이 "밤에 일어나는 사소한 일" (the little thing that happens at night)이라고 말하는 도중 말을 가로챈다.

Shrek과 당나귀가 DuLoc의 Farquaad 궁전에 도착할 무렵 이곳에서는 호위병들간에 시합이 벌어지고 있었다. 승자는 용암에 둘러싸여있는 성안에서 불을 내뿜는 용이 보호하고 있는 Finona를 구출하는 "영광"을 누리게 된다. Shrek은 시합을 손쉽게 이기고 Farquaad는 그가 Fiona를 구해오면 늪에서 조무래기들이 물러나도록 해 주겠다고 약속한다.

Shrek과 당나귀가 드디어 장도에 오른다. 당나귀는 특유의 입담을 활용 암컷인 용의 맘에 들게 된다. Shrek은 Fiona를 찾아내지만 Fiona는 자신을 대하는 그의 태도에 실망한다. 백마탄 멋진 기사가 나타나 공주인 자신을 구해줄 것을 기대했기 때문이다. 절박한 상황에서 Shrek은 Fiona와 당나귀를 천신만고 끝에 구해낸다. 궁중으로 가는 도중 Fiona는 Shrek이 헬멧을 벗자 괴물이라는 사실을 뒤늦게 깨닫고 더욱 실망한다. 그러나 Shrek은 Fiona과 자신이 공통점이 많다고 느끼면서 연정을 느낀다. 그런데 Fiona는 해가 저물면 동굴 속으로 들어가 혼자 지내는 이상한 행동을 한다. Shrek은 늪으로 돌아가면 주변에 담장을 두를 것이라 말하면서 세상에 대한 원망을 드러낸다. 사람들이 자기를 알아보려고 하기도 전에 판단을 내려 버리기 때문이라는 것이다.

다음날 밤 당나귀는 Fiona가 요괴로 변한 모습을 보게 된다. Fiona는 자신이 어렸을 때 저주를 받아 밤만 되면 요괴로 변하는데 진정으로 자신을 사랑하는 사람의 키스만이 본래의 모습으로 되돌려 준다고 고백한다. 그 즈음 Shrek은 Fiona에게 자신의 사랑을 고백할 참이었는데 뜻밖에 Fiona와 당나귀의 대화에서 흘러나온 "추한 야수" 로의 변신을 증오한다는 말을 엿듣는다. Fiona가 자신이 밤만 되면 입버릇처럼 말하는 요괴가 되는 신세한탄하는 것을 자신을 깎아내리는 소리로 오해한 것이다. 낙담한 Shrek은 Fiona를 Farquaad에게 구해주는 임무를 마치고 쓸쓸히 늪으로 돌아온다.

늪에서의 Shrek은 허탈한 나머지 애꿏은 당나귀를 구박한다. 당나귀는 Fiona에 대한 Shrek의 오해를 풀도록 하고 곧 결혼식을 올리게 될 Fiona를 정말 사랑한다면 결혼식을 중단시킬 것을 주문한다. 어제의 원수에서 이제는 친구가 된 거대한 몸집을 가진 용의 도움을 받아 Duloc 궁전으로 날아가 Farquaad가 Fiona에게 사랑의 키스를 하기 직전에 식을 중단시킨다. 하지만 때가 해가 진 이후였기 때문에 Fiona는 요괴로 변한 뒤였다. 이 모습을 본 Farquaad는 Fiona를 감옥에 가두도록 하지만 이 순간 용이 들이닥쳐 Farquaad를 삼켜버린다. Shrek과 Fiona는 서로의 사랑을 확인하고 Fiona는 휘황찬란한 불빛 아래에서 이상하게도 요괴의 모습으로 남아 있는다. Shrek은 실망하는 Fiona를 진정시키고 주위의 축복 속에 늪에서 결혼식을 올리고 부부가 된다.

❊ Preview

Give me another chance.

한 번 봐주세요.

I bet! You bet!

확실하지.

My patience has **reached its end.**

내 인내심이 한계가 이르렀지.

The first **runner up**, second runner up…

차점자, 차차점자

Let me **get** this **straight.**

똑바로 바로 잡겠습니다.

That money **will do** me for the present.

당분간 그 돈이면 돼.

To him you are **pain in the neck.**

그 사람에 너는 눈에 가시야.

This is coffee **of a kind.**

커피도 커피 나름이지.

The lion **charged towards** its prey.

사자가 먹잇감을 향해 돌진했다.

I'm **on the road** a lot. You are **off the road** in winter.

저는 자주 집을 비웁니다. 겨울에는 집에 머물죠.

I'm not your type.

저와 다르신 것 같아요.

The boy **made up the story.**

그 아이가 그 얘기를 지어낸 거야.

Your words **cut** him **deep**.

네 말이 그에게 깊은 상처를 줬지.

I want to **make it up** to you.

벌충해 줄게.

I'**m coming**!

예 가요.

The peasant is **yanking out** the weed from his paddy field,

농부가 논에서 잡초를 뽑고 있습니다.

They are **digging on** each other.

그 사람들은 서로 좋아해.

The service is provided to you **24/7**.

하루 24시간 휴일 없이 영업합니다.

You've **got a lot in common**.

너희들은 공통점이 많군.

Never been better.

이 이상 좋을 수 없지.

Round up some guests.

손님들을 동원해 와.

They'll **make it** in time.

그들은 정시에 도착할 거야.

Dialogue

(narration) Once upon a time there was a lovely princess. But she had an enchantment upon her of a fearful sort, which could only be broken by Love's first kiss ….

1. Shrek as an Ogre

MAN 1 Think it's in there.

MAN 2 All right. **Let's get it**!

MAN 3 Hold on. You know what it could do to you?

MAN 4 Yeah. It'll grind your bones for its bread.

SHREK Yes, well, actually, that would be a giant. Now ogres are much worse. They'll make a suit from your freshly peeled skin…
They'll shave your liver, squeeze the jelly from your eyes! Actually, it's quite good at toast.

2. A Flying, Talking Donkey

GUARD Right, this one is full. Take it away. Give me that.

TAX COLLECTOR Your flying days are over. That's 25 pieces of sliver for the witch.

GUARD Next. Get up.

GUARD Sit down there! Keep quite!

BEAR This cage is too small.

DONKEY Please don't turn me in. I'll never be stubborn again. I can change.
Please, **give me another chance**.

……

TAX COLLECTOR That's good for ten shillings, if you can prove it.

OLD WOMAN He's just, he's just nervous. He's really quite a chatter box. Talk, you **boneheaded** dolt!

TAX COLLECTOR That's it. I have heard enough. Guards!

OLD WOMAN No, no, he talks, he does. I can talk. I love to talk. I'm the talking damn thing you ever saw….

TAX COLLECTOR Guards, get her out of my sight!

……

GUARDS He can fly! He can fly!

TAX COLLECTOR He can talk!

DONKEY That's right. Fool! Now I'm a flying, talking donkey! You might have seen a house fly., maybe even a super fly. But **I bet** you ain't never seen a donkey fly!

3. Donkey Came Across Shrek

GUARD You there, orgre!

SHREK Aye?

GUARD By the order of Loard Farquaad, I am authorized to place you both under arrest. And transport you to a designated resettlement facility.

SHREK Oh, really? You and what army?

DONKEY Can I say something to you? Listen you was really, really something back there. Incredible!

……

If you don't mind me saying, if that don't work, your breath certainly will get the job done, 'cause you definitely need some **Tic Tacs**[17] or something, cause our breath stinks!

4. Uninvited Guests in the Swamp

MOUSE Well, gents. It is far cry from the farm, but what choice do we have?

MOUSE It's not···home, but it'll do just fine.

MOUSE What a lovely bed!

---

[17] *Tic Tacs*: a breath mint

SHREK	Got you!
	……
	Oh, no! No, no! What are you doing in my swamp? All right. **Get out of here**. All of you. Move it! Come on, let's go. Hapaya, hapaya···No, no, not there. Not there!
DONKEY	Hey don't look at me. I didn't invite them.
	……
PIG	He huffed und puffed und he signed an eviction notice.
SHREK	All right. Who knows where this Farquaad guy is?
DONKEY	Oh I do. I know where he is.
SHREK	Does anyone else know where to find him? Anyone at all?
	……
SHREK	In fact, I'm gonna see this guy Fraquaad right now, and get you all off my land. And back where you came from!
DONKEY	Shrek and Donkey, two stalwart friends off on a whirlwind big-city adventure.

5. Lord Farquaad

LORD FARQUAAD	Run, Run, Run as fast as you can. You can't catch me. I'm the ginger bread man!
GINGERBREAD	You're monster. I'm not the monster here.
LORD FARQUAAD	You and rest of that fairy tale trash are poisoning my perfect world.
	……
LORD FARQUAAD	I've tried to be fair to you creatures. **Now my patience has reached its end**! Tell me! Or I'll···.
GINGERBREAD	Man, no, no, but the buttons. Not my gumdrop buttons.
LORD FARQUAAD	All right! Who's hiding them?
	……
SOLDIER	My lord! We found it.
LORD FARQUAAD	Well then, what are you waiting for? Bring it in. Magic mirror.
GINGERBREAD	Don't tell him anything!
	……
MAGIC MIRROR	What I mean is a ···you're not a king yet. But you can become one. All you have to do is marry a princess.
LORD FARQUAAD	Go on.

……

MAGIC MIRROR Bachelorette number two is a cape wearing girl from a land of fantasy. Although she lives with seven other men, she is not easy. Just kiss her dead frozen lips and find out what a live wife she is. Come on. Give it up for···Snow-White. And last, but certainly not least, bachelorette no 3 is a fiery redhead from a dragon-guarded castle surrounded by hot boiling lava! But don't let that cool you off!

……

LORD FARQUAAD You've chosen···Princess Fiona.

LORD FARQUAAD She's nice. Fiona. She's perfect. All I have to do is just find someone···

MAGIC MIRROR But I probably should mention little thing that happens at night···

LORD FARQUAAD I'll do it!

❊ Review

Let's get it!
잡자.

Give me another chance.
한 번만 봐주세요.

Boneheaded, egg headed, bigheaded…
멍텅구리.

I bet you are right.
네가 옳다고 확신해.

You bet!
두 말할 것 없지!

My patience has reached its end.
인내심이 한계에 도달했다.

All you have to do is to focus on the game.
오로지 경기에 집중하는 거야.

❇ Activity 3-1

I. Try it on in English.

1. 한번만 기회를 더 주십시오.

2. 그 책이 베스트셀러가 되는 것은 장담해.

3. 나에게 당시 선택의 여지가 없었다.

4. 공자님의 인내심도 한계에 도달했다.

5. 네가 해야 할 일은 아이를 돌보는 것이다.

II. Answer the given questions and develop your idea.

1. What do you think of the main character Shrek's personality?

2. Can you define Lord Farquaad as a proper leader of people?

III. Words to Live By.

1. All's well that ends well.

2. Blood is thicker than water.

3. You can't make omelet without breaking eggs.

4. What can't be cured must be endured.

Dialogue

6. Shrek Won the Tournament

SHREK All right. You're going to the right way for a smacked bottom.

DONKEY Sorry about that.

LORD FARQUAAD That champion should have the honor, o, no···. the privilege to go forth and rescue the lovely princess Fiona from the firing keep of the dragon. If for any reason that winner is unsuccessful, **the first runner up** will take his place. Andso on, and so forth. Some of you may die, but it's a sacrifice I'm willing to make.

……

SOLDIER Shall I give the order sir?

LORD FARQUAAD No. I have a better idea. People of DuLoc. I give you our champion!

SHREK What?

LORD FARQUAAD Congratulations, Ogre. You've won the honor of embarking on a great and noble quest.

SHREK Quest? I'm already on a quest. A quest to get my swamp back!

LORD FARQUAAD Your swamp?

SHREK Yeah, my swamp! Where you **dumped** those fairy tale creatures.

FARQUAAD Indeed. All right, ogre, **I'll make you a deal**. Go on this quest for me, and I'll give your swamp back.

SHREK Exactly the way it was?

FARQUAAD Down to the last slime-covered toad stool···.

7. Ogres Have Layers

DONKEY OK, **let me get this straight**! You're gonna go find the dragon and rescue a princess if just so Farquaad will give you back the swamp, which you only don't have, 'cause he filled it with full of freaks on the first place. Is that about right?

SHREK You know what? Maybe there is a good reason, donkeys shouldn't talk.

DONKEY I don't get it Shrek. Why didn't you just pull some ogre stuff on him? You know, throttle him, lay siege to his fortress. Grind his bones to make a bread, the whole ogre trip.

SHREK Oh, I know what. Maybe I could have decapitated an entire village and put their heads on a pike, gotten a knife, cut open their spleen and drink their fluids. Does that sound good to you?

DONKEY A, no, not really, no.

SHREK For your information, there's a lot more to ogres than people think.

……

SHREK Ogres have layers! Ogres have layers.

……

I don't care what everyone likes. Ogres are not like cakes.

DONKEY You know what everyone likes? **Parfait**[18]**.** Have you ever met a person and you say: Hey, let's get some parfait and they say I don't like parfait. Parfait is delicious.

SHREK No! You dense, irritating, miniature beast of burden. Ogres are like onions. End of story. Bye bye. See you later.

DONKEY Parfaits maybe the most delicious thing on the whole damn planet.

SHREK You know I think I've preferred you humming.

DONKEY Do you have a tissue or something, 'cause I'm making a mess. Just the word parfait makes me start **slobbering**[19].

……

SHREK Believe me donkey if it was me, you'd be dead. It's brimstone. We must be getting close.

DONKEY Yeah, right, brimstone. Don't be talking about brimstone. I know what I smell and it wasn't no brimstone. And it comes off no stone neither.

SHREK Sure it's big enough, but look at the location.

DONKEY Oh, Shrek, remember when you said that ogres have layers?

SHREK Oh, yeah. All right.

DONKEY Well, I have a better confession to make. Donkeys don't have layers. We wear our fear on our sleeves.

SHREK Wait a second. Donkeys don't have sleeves.

DONKEY You know what I mean.

……

---

[18] *parfait*: a dessert of ice cream and fruit or ice cream and syrup in alternate layers, often topped with whipped cream.

[19] *slobber*: to let saliva run from the mouth.

DONKEY	I'm just uncomfortable about being on a **rickety**[20] bridge over a boiling lake of lava. Shrek, Come on donkey, I'm right here beside you. OK? For emotional support. We'll just tackle this thing together one little baby step at a time.
DONKEY	Really?
SHREK	Really, really.
DONKEYOK	That makes me feel so much better.
SHREK	Just keep moving and don't look down.
DONKEY	Don't look down, don't look down. Keep on moving, Don't look down. Keep on moving. Shrek! I'm looking down! Oh, God. I can't do this. Just let me off, please.

……

DONKEY	I'm gonna die. I'm gonna die. Shrek, I'm gonna die.
SHREK	That will do, donkey. **That will do**.
DONKEY	Cool. So where is this fire breathing **pain in the neck** anyway?
SHREK	Inside.Waiting for us to rescue her.

8. The Dragon's Keep

SHREK	The princess will be up the stairs in the highest room in the tallest tower.
DONKEY	What makes you think she'll be there?
SHREK	I read it in a book once.
DONKEY	Cool. You handle the dragon. I'll **handle** the stairs. Oh, I'll find those stairs. I'll whip their butt, too. That's right. Those stairs won't know which way they're going. Take a drastic steps. Kick it to the curb. Don't mess with me. I'm the stair master. I've mastered the stairs. I wish I had a step right here right now, I'd step all over it.

……

Oh, what large teeth you have.I mean, I mean, white sparkling teeth. I know you probably hear this all the time from your food, but you must bleach yourself, because that is one dazzling smile you got there. And do I detect the hint of minty freshness? And you know what else? You're a girl dragon! Oh,sure. Of course, you're a girl dragon, cause you're just reeking the feminine beauty out. What's the matter with you? Do you

[20]*rickety*: likely to fall or collapse; shaky: a rickety chair.

have something in your eye? Man, I'd really love to stay, but you know I'm an asthmatic and I don't know if it'd worked out if you're blowing smoke rings.

9. The Rescue Operations

SHREK Wake up!

FIONA What?

SHREK Are you Princess Fiona?

FIONA I'm awaiting for a knight so bold to rescue me.

SHREK Oh, that's nice. Let's go!

FIONA But wait, Sir Knight. This be-ith our first meeting. Should it not be a wonderful, romantic moment?

SHREK Yeah, sorry, lady. There is no time.

FIONA Hey, wait. What are you doing? You should sweep me off my feet out yonder Window and down a rope onto your valiant steed.

SHREK You've had a lot of time to plan this, haven't you?

……

FIONA But we have to **savor** this moment! You could recite an epic poem for me. A ballad! A Sonnet! A limerick! Or something!

SHREK I don't think so. Can I at least know the name of my champion?

SHREK Shrek!

FIONA I pray that you take this favor as a token of my gratitude.

……

You didn't slay the dragon? You were meant to **charge in**, sword drawn, banner flying. That's what all the other Knights did.

SHREK Yeah, right before they burst into flame.

……

FIONA What kind of knight are you?

SHREK **One of a kind**.

DONKEY I don't want to rush into physical relationship. I'm not that emotionally ready for commitment of this magnitude, really. That was the word I was looking for, magnitude. Hey, that is unwanted physical contact. Hey, what are you doing? OK, OK, Listen. Let's just back up a little and take this one step at a time. I mean, we really should get to know each other first as friends or pen pals. I'm **on the road** a lot, but I just love receiving cards···, Hey don't do that.That's my tail. And you're gonna tear it off··· I don't give permission.What are you going to do with that? Hey now, no way.

❊ Review

The **first runner up**, second runner up…

차점자, 차차점자

He **dumped** his girl friend.

그 친구 여자 친구를 버렸어.

I'll **make** you **a deal**.

협상을 해 보지.

Keep going.

계속해.

The staff **handled** it nicely.

그 직원이 그 일을 잘 처리했지.

Smoke **curled from** the chimney.

굴뚝에서 연기가 모락모락 피어 올랐다.

This is coffee **of a kind**; He is a gentleman **of a kind**.

커피도 커피 나름이지. 신사도 신사나름이자.

The lion **charged towards** its prey.

사자가 먹잇감을 향해 돌진했다.

I'm **on the road** a lot. You are **off the road** in winter.

외유 중인 경우가 많다. 겨울에 집에 머문다.

I'm not **emotionally ready** for something.

저 어떤 일 할 마음의 준비가 덜 돼 있습니다.

We have to **savor** this moment.

이 순간을 즐겨야죠.

Music Break

Simon and Garfunkle : Bridge Over Troubled Water

(Don't trouble the water)
I won't
(Give it up)
(Why don't you, why don't you, let it be?)
Um hum
(Still water run deep, yes it do)
I know that
(Whoa yeah)
Yeah, if you only believe

(Don't trouble the water)
Said I wouldn't
(Give it up)
(Why don't you, why don't you, let it be?)
Umm
(Still water run deep)
Yes it do
(Yes it do whoa oh ho yeah)
If you only believe

When you're down now
When you're on the street
When evenin' falls
Somehow I will comfort you

I'll take the bow
Whoa when darkness comes
And your love around
Just like a bridge over troubled water
I will lay me down
(Like a bridge)
Just like a bridge
(Over troubled)
Over troubled water
I will lay me down

Sail on silver moon
Sail on by
Your time has come to shine
All of your dreams are on their way
(See how they shine?)

Ooh and if you ever need a friend
(Need a friend)
Look around and sailing by
Just like a bridge over troubled water
I'll be there to lay me down
(Like a bridge)
Like a bridge over
(Troubled water)
Troubled water
I will lay me down
Ooh, I'll be your bridge
Yes I will

(Don't trouble the water)
Said I wouldn't
(Give it up)

Well
(Why don't you, why don't you, let it be?)
Uh huh
(Still water run deep)
I know that
(Yes it do)
Yeah
(Oh yeah)

Still the water
(Don't trouble the water)
Yeah
(Give it up, why don't you, why don't you, let it be?)
Talkin' 'bout still water
(Still water run deep)
You know they run deep
(Yes it do)
Uh huh
(Oh yeah)

Well I'm gonna be your bridge yeah
(Don't trouble the water)
The troubled water
(Give it up)
Oh
(Why don't you, why don't you, let it be?)
Come on come on
Walk out on me
(Still water run deep)
Oh
(Yes it do)

❊ Activity 3-2

I.Try it on in English.

1. 협상 합시다.

2. 그 여직원은 일 처리를 잘해.

3. 부모도 부모 나름이지.

4. 치타가 영양을 향해 돌진하고 있다.

5. 저 일 시작할 마음의 준비가 덜 돼 있습니다.

6. 순간을 즐겨라.

II. Answer the given questions and develop your idea.

1. Shrek accomplished his mission to rescue Princess Fiona at the risk of his life. Can you compare Shrek and donkey facing a critical moment?

2. How did the donkey get out of the imminent crisis when he bumped into the dragon to kill him?

III. Words We Live By

1. You can educate a fool, but you cannot make him think.

2. Who is wise? One who learns from all.

3. Life is so short we must move very slowly.

4. The highest form of wisdom is kindness.

Dialogue

10. After the Job Done

FIONA	The battle is won. You may remove your helmet, good Sir Knight.
SHREK	I have helmet hair.
FIONA	Please.I would'st look upon the face of my rescuer.
SHREK	No. You wouldn't.
FIONA	But how will you kiss me?
SHREK	What? That wasn't in the job description.
DONKEY	Maybe it's a **perk**[21].
FIONA	Not, it's destiny. Oh, you must know how it goes….

……

PRINCESS FIONA	What is so funny?
SHREK	Let's just say **I'm not your type**, OK?
PRINCESS FIONA	Of course, you are. You're rescuer. Now remove your helmet.
SHREK	Look. I'm really don't think this is a good idea.
PRINCESS FIONA	Just **take off** the helmet.
SHREK	I'm not going to.
PRINCESS FIONA	Take it off!

……

SHREK	OK. Easy. As you command, your Highness.
PRINCESS FIONA	You're an ogre!!!
SHREK	Oh, you were expecting Prince Charming.
PRINCESS FIONA	Well, yes actually. No. This is all wrong. You're not supposed to be an ogre.
SHREK	Princess, I was sent to rescue you by Lord Farquaad, OK? He's the one Who wants to marry you.

……

PRINCESS FIONA	Put me down, or you will suffer the consequences! This is not dignified. Put me down.
DONKEY	OK, here's another question. Say there's that woman that **digs** you, but you don't really like her that way. How do you let her down real easy?

---

[21]*perk*: perquisite: special gratitude

So her feeling aren't hurt, but you don't get burned to a crisp and eaten? How would you do that?

PRINCESS FIONA Just tell her, she's not your true love. Everyone knows what happens, When you find your······The sooner we get to DuLoc, the better.

DONKEY You gonna love it there, Princess. It's beautiful.

PRINCESS FIONA And what of my-groom-to-be? Lord Farquaad? What's he like?

11. Under the Starry Sky

SHREK You can guess what he's famous for?

DONKEY Now I know you're **making this up**.

SHREK No. Look. There he is and there's a group of hunters running away from the stench.

DONKEY That ain't nothing, but a bunch of little dots.

SHREK You know donkey, sometimes things are more than they appear. Forget it.

DONKEY Hey, Shrek. What are you gonna do when we get our swamp back, anyway?

SHREK Our swamp?

DONKEY You know. When we're through with rescuing the princess and all that stuff.

SHREK The first thing I'm gonna do is build a ten-foot wall around my land.

DONKEY You **cut me deep** I think this whole wall thing is just a way to keep somebody out.

......

DONKEY Oh, now we're getting somewhere.

SHREK Oh, **for 'the love of pete'**[22]

DONKEY Hey, what's your problem, Shrek? What do you got against whole world, anyway?

SHREK Look. I'm not the one with the problem. OK? It's the world that seems to have a problem with me. People take one look at me and go. A···Help! A big stupid ugly ogre. They judge me before they even know me. That's why I'**m better off** alone.

---

[22]*for the love of pete*: a euphemism for "for the love of God" and "for pity's sake".

❊ Review

I'm not your type.

저는 당신과 다른 사람입니다.

Take off the cap. Put on the cap.

탈모 하세요. 모자 쓰세요.

The woman **digs** the gentleman.

그 여성은 그 남성을 좋아해.

It **takes time** to end the work.

일 마치는데 시간이 좀 걸려.

The boy **made up** the story.

그 아이가 이야기를 꾸며낸 거야.

We're through.

우린 끝났어.

The teacher is **better off** at the school.

그 선생님은 학교에 있는 것이 나아.

Your words **cut** him **deep**.

네 말이 그 사람에게 큰 상처를 준거야.

❊ Activity 3-3

I. Try it on in English.

1. 나는 그 대회에서 차점자였다.

2. 이해가 안되네요.

3. 누가 뭐라고 해도 상관 안 해.

4. 두 사람은 요즘 사이가 좋아지고 있다.

5. 그 일을 시작할 마음의 준비를 해!

6. 나 좀 내려줘!

7. 나는 혼자 지내는 것이 나아.

II. Answer the given questions and develop your idea.

1.What was the first response of Princess Fiona when she found Shrek was an ogre?

2.What do you think of Donkey as one of characters in this film? What is its relation to Shrek?

III. Words to Live by.

1. In at one ear and out at the other.

2. Familiarity bleeds contempt.

3. Those who sow wind, shall reap the whirlwind.

4. To every thing, there is a season.

Dialogue

12. Fiona, Karate Woman

PRINCESS FIONA Good morning. How do you like your eggs?

DONKEY Good morning, princess.

SHREK What's all this about?

PRINCESS FIONA You know, we kind of got off to a bad start yesterday and I wanted to **make it up** to you. I mean. After all, you did rescue me.

SHREK Thanks.

PRINCESS FIONA Well, eat up. We've got a big day ahead of us.

……

SHREK What? It's a compliment. Better out than in, I always say.

DONKEY But it's no way to behave in front of a princess.

PRINCESS FIONA Thanks.

DONKEY She's as nasty as you are.

SHREK You know. You're not exactly what I've expected.

……

DONKEY You can't do this to me. Shrek's too young to die. Keep your legs elevated.Turn your head and cough. Does anyone know the **Heimlich**[23]**?** ….

SHREK Donkey! Calm down.

PRINCESS FIONA If you want to help Shrek, run into woods and find me a blue flower with

---

[23]*Heimlich maneuver*:

red thorns.

DONKEY Blue flowers, red thorns. OK. I'm on it. Blue flower, red thorns. Blue flower, red thorns. Don't die Shrek. And if you see a long tunnel, stay away from the light!

SHREK AND PRINCESS FIONA Donkey!

DONKEY Oh, yeah. Right. Blue flower, red thorns. Blue flower, red thorns.

SHREK What are the flowers for?

PRINCESS FIONA For getting rid of Donkey. Now, you hold still and I'll yank this thing out.

……

DONKEY Blue flower, red thorns.Blue flower, red thorns. Blue flower, red throns. This would be so much easier if I wasn't color blind. Blue flower, red thorns.blue flower, red thorns. Hold on, Shrek. **I'm coming**.

13. Digging on Each Other

SHREK Well, they also great in stews. Now, I don't mean to brag, but I make a mean weedrat stew.

PRINCESS FIONA I guess I'll be dining a little differently tomorrow night.

SHREK Maybe you can come visit me in the swamp sometime. I'll cook all kinds of stuff for you. Swamp taud soup, fish eye tartare, **you name it**.

……

DONKEY Ahh. Now, I really see what's going on here.

SHREK Oh, what are you talking about?

DONKEY Hey, I don't wanna even hair. Look, I'm an animal and I got instincts. And I know that you **two are digging on each other**.I could feel it.

SHREK Oh, you're crazy. I'm just bring her back to Farquaad.

14. Ogress Fiona

DONKEY Princess. Princess Fiona? Princess, where are you? Princess? It's very **spooky** in here and I ain't playing no games. No, no. Help! Shrek! Shrek! No, Shrek!

……

FIONA When I was a little girl, a witch cast a spell on me. Every night I become this. This horrible ugly beast! I was placed in a tower to await

	the day my true love would rescue me. That's why I have to marry Lord Farquaad tomorrow before the sunsets and he sees me, like this.
DONKEY	All right, all right. Calm down. Look, it's not that bad. You're not that ugly. Wait, I ain't gonna lie. You are ugly. But you only look like this at night. Shrek's ugly **24/7**.
PRINCESS FIONA	But Donky. I'm a princess. And this is not how a princess is meant to look.
DONKEY	Princess. How about if you don't marry Farquaad?
PRINCESS FIONA	I have to. Only my true love's kiss can break the spell.
DONKEY	But you know, you're kind of an ogre And Shrek… Well, **you've got a lot in common**.

15. Handed it Over

FIONA	Are you all right?
SHREK	Perfect. **Never been better**.
PRINCESS FIONA	There's something I have to tell you.
SHREK	You don't have to tell me anything, princess. I heard enough last night.
PRINCESS FIONA	You've heard what I said?
SHREK	Every word.
PRINCESS FIONA	I thought you'd understand?
SHREK	Oh, I understand! Like you said, who could love a hideous, ugly beast?
PRINCESS FIONA	I thought that wouldn't matter to you.
	……
LORD FARQUAAD	Oh. That is so sweet. You don't have to waste good manners on the ogre. It's not like it has feelings.
PRINCESS FIONA	No. You're right. It doesn't.
LORD FARQUAAD	Princess Fiona, beautiful fair **flawless** Fiona, I ask your hand in marriage. Will you be the perfect bride for the perfect groom?
	……
PRINCESS FIONA	No! I mean I… Why wait? Let's get married today. Before sunset.
LORD FARQUAAD	Oh, how anxious we are? You're right. The sooner the better. That's so much to do. Yes, the cake, the band, the guests…Captain! **Round up** some guests.
PRINCESS FIONA	Fare-thee-well, ogre.
	……

SHREK Yeah I know you talked to her last night. You're great pal, aren't you? Now, if you two are such good friends, why don't you follow her home?

DONKEY Shrek. I want to go with you.

SHREK I told you, didn't I? You're not coming home with me. I live alone. My swamp, me, nobody else! Understand? Nobody! Especially useless, **pathetic**[24], annoying, talking donkeys!

DONKEY But. I thought…..

SHREK Yeah. You know what? You thought wrong.

16. That's What Friends are for

SHREK Fine!

DONKEY Hey, hey, come back here. I'm not through with you, yet.

SHREK Well, **I'm through with you**!

DONKEY Well, you know. You were always "Me, me, me! Well, guess. What? Now it's my turn! So you just shut up and pay attention! You are **mean to** me, you insult me, you don't appreciate anything I do! You're always pushing me, around or pushing me away.

SHREK Oh, yeah? If I treated you so bad, how come you came back?

DONKEY Because that's what friend do. They forgive each other!

SHREK Oh, yeah. You're right, donkey. I forgive you for **stabbing me in the back.**

DONKEY Oh! You're so wrapped up in layers, onion boy, you're afraid of your own feelings.

……

DONKEY Hey, that's what friends are for, right?

SHREK Right, Friends?

DONKEY Friends.

SHREK So? What did Fiona say about me?

DONKEY What are you asking me for? Why don't you just go ask her?

SHREK The wedding! We'll never **make it in time**!

DONKEY Never fear! For where there is a will, there is a way. And I have a way.

---

[24] *pathetic*: causing or evoking pity, sympathetic sadness, sorrow, etc.

17. Groom Shrek

DONKEY There's a line you gotta wait for. The preacher's gonna say, "Speak now, or forever hold your peace." That's what you say, "I object."

……

All right. Cut it out. When does this guy say the line?

DONKEY We got to **check it out**.

THE REVEREND And as so by the power vested in me.

SHREK What do you see?

THE REVEREND I now pronounce you husband and wife.….

DONKEY They are at the alter. He already said it.

SHREK Oh! For 'the love of pete' " I object!!!"

……

LORD FARQUAAD Oh, this is precious. The ogre has fallen in love with the princess.

All (Laugh)

FIONA Shrek. Is this true?

LORD FARQUAAD **Who cares? It's preposterous**. Fiona, my love, we're but a kiss away for our happily ever after. Now kiss me!

……

SHREK Well, that explains a lot.

LORD FARQUAAD Oh. It's disgusting. Guards, guards. I order you to get them out of my sight. Now! Get them! Get them! Get them, both!

……

DONKEY All right. Nobody move! I got a dragon here and I'm not afraid to use it. I'm a donky on the edge! Celebrity marriages. They never last, do they? Go ahead, Shrek.

……

PRINCESS FIONA Yes. But I don't understand. I'm supposed to be beautiful.

SHREK But you are beautiful.

DONKEY I was hoping this would be a happy ending.

❊ Review

I want to **make it up** to you.
여러분 그 것 벌충해 드릴게요.

I'm coming!
예 가요.

The peasant is **yanking** out the weed from his paddy field.
농부가 논에서 잡초를 뽑고 있다.

It's very **spooky** here.
여기 정말 무섭다.

The service is provided to you 24/7.
하루 24시간 휴일 없이 영업

You've **got a lot in common.**
너희들 공통점이 많구나.

Never been better.
이 이상 좋을 수는 없지.

Round up some guests.
손님들 좀 동원해 오시오.

She has **flawless** character.
흠잡을 데 없는 성격이다.

I'm through with you.
당신과 끝났어.

You stabbed me in the back.
뒤에서 비수를 들이댔지.

Everything's here, you name it.

다 있습니다. 뭐든지.

You have been mean to me.

너 나에게 못되게 굴었지.

They'll make it in time.

그 사람들 정시에 올 거야.

When does this guy say the line?

이 친구 이 글귀 언제 읊나?

We got to **check it out.**

확인해 봐야 돼.

Who cares?

알게 뭐람?

It's preposterous.

말도 안돼.

You name it!

그 밖에 뭐든지!

❊ Activity 3-4

I. Try it on in English.

1. 국수를 어떻게 끓여 드릴까요?

2. 당신과 화해하고 싶소.

3. 오늘은 내게 중요한 날이다.

4. 지금 가고 있습니다.

5. 이름들을 대 보세요.

6. 그 가게는 항상 열려 있다.

7. 당신과 당장 결혼하고 싶어요.

8. 그 사람은 관중동원에 능하다.

9. 제 차례예요.

10. 그 사람은 제 시간에 못 해낼 거야.

11 저 친구는 위험한 인물이야.

II. Answer the given questions and develop your idea.

1. Why did Princess Fiona want to marry Lord Farquaad before sunset?

2. What happened to Shrek at the end of the story? What do you think about the ending?

III. Words to Live by

1. First come, first served.

2. Soil and friendship must be cultivated.

3. Truth is stranger than fiction.

4. Two is company, three's a crowd.

Music Break

Movie Avatar : I See You

I see you
I see you

Walking through a dream
I see you
My light in darkness breathing hope of new life
Now I live through you and you through me
Enchanting
I pray in my heart that this dream never ends

I see me through your eyes
Living through life flying high
Your life shines the way into paradise
So I offer my life as a sacrifice
I live through your love

You teach me how to see
All that's beautiful
My senses touch your word I never pictured
Now I give my hope to you
I surrender
I pray in my heart that this world never ends

I see me through your eyes
Living through life flying high

Your love shines the way into paradise
So I offer my life
I offer my love, for you

When my heart was never open
(and my spirit never free)
To the world that you have shown me
But my eyes could not division
All the colours of love and of life ever more
Evermore

(I see me through your eyes)
I see me through your eyes
(Living through life flying high)
Flying high
Your love shines the way into paradise
So I offer my life as a sacrifice
And live through your love
And live through your life

I see you
I see you

4. The Emperor's New Groove

2000년 Walt Disney사 제작 코미디 애니메이션 영화. 제목 The Emperor's New Groove는 덴마크 동화 The Emperor's New Clothes의 제목을 따온 것이다. 내용은 뮤지컬 King of the Sun과 유사하다.

Plot

잉카제국의 자기 밖에 모르는 꼬마 황제 Kuzco는 인근 마을의 촌장 Pacha를 불러들인다. 이름하여 Kuzcotopia라는 거창한 여름별장을 Pacha가 사는 마을에 짓겠다는 것이다. 황제의 간교하고 권력을 탐해온 측근 Yzma여인과 보디가드 Kronk는 Kuzco를 독살한 다음 Yzma가 권좌를 차지하려 음모를 꾸민다. 그러나 Kronk가 잘못 선택한 독약을 먹은 황제는 죽지 않고 llama가 된다.

Yzma는 브로콜리 한 사발로 Kuzco를 기절시켜 마을 밖에서 끝내 버리도록 Kronk를 사주한다. 그러나 양심의 가책을 느낀 Kronk는 우연찮게 Kuzco를 놓친다. Pacha마을에 당도한 Kuzco는 Pacha가 자신을 llama로 만든 장본인이라고 착각하고 궁중에 되돌아갈 수 있도록 애걸한다. Pacha는 여름별장 계획을 철회하면 도와주겠다고 제안하지만 Kuzco는 듣지 않고 길을 떠나 우글거리는 Jaguar 떼를 만나 생명이 위태로울 찰나 Pacha의 도움으로 겨우 목숨을 부지한다. 그 즈음 Yzma는 천하를 호령하지만 Kronk가 Kuzco 암살에 실패했다는 말을 듣고 둘은 Kuzco 를 찾아내 요절을 내기위해 길을 나선다.

Kuzco와 Pacha는 궁중으로 가는 길에 한 식당에 들른다. 잠시 후 Yzma와 Kronk가 도착한다. Pacha는 이들이 Kuzco 살해계획을 모의하는 것을 엿듣고 Kuzco에게 알려준다. 하지만 아직도 Yzma가 자신의 충성파로 착각하고 Pacha를 되레 비난한다. 그러나 Yzma와 Kronk이 자신을 죽이려 한다는 둘 간의 대화를 엿듣고 비로소 Pacha를 믿게 된다. 이미 Pacha가 떠난 뒤이다. 얼마 후 이들은 화해하고 둘은 Pacha의 집에 들른다. 이 때 이곳에는 Kuzco를 찾아내려는 Yzma와 Kronk가 와 있음을 눈치채게 된다. Pacha의 아내 Chlcha의 기지로 이 곳을 탈출하지만 오래지 않아 Yzma와 Kronk가 멀리 시야에서 사리지고 있는 Pacha와 Kuzco 일행을 발견하고 추격하기 시작한다. Kuzco일행은 계곡에 이르러 거의 따라 잡힐 순간 날아서 계곡을 건너던 Yzma와 Kronk는 벼락을 맞고 계곡 아래로 떨어져 Pacha와 Kuzco는 위기를 모면한다.

그러나 Kuzco와 Pacha가 서둘러 Yzama의 실험실에 도착해 보니 이상하게도 Yzma와 Kronk이 먼저 도착해 있다. 이 때 Kronk은 자신의 요리를 타박하는 Yzma를 배반하고 샨델리어 줄을 끊어 Yzma를 죽이려 하지만 샨델리어는 몸이 실처럼 가는 Yzma 몸을 맞추지 못하고 만다. 물약병을 놓고 일 대 뺏고 빼앗기는 혼전이 벌어진 후 Pacha와 Kuzco는 2개의 물약병을 손에 넣게 되나 Yzma가 그 중 하나를 차지하여 작은 고양이로 변신한다. 드디어 두 물약병 중 Kuzco가 사람으로 환원될 수 있는 해독제를 차지하여 소원대로 Kuzco는 인간으로 재탄생하여 Pacha의 집 옆에 작은 여름별장을 짓는다. Kronk는 고양이가 된 Yzma가 단원으로 있는 다람쥐 스카우트단장으로 일하게 된다.

❊ Preview

He looks really **pathetic**.
그 사람 정말 처량하게 보이네.

Trot out your best dress.
어디 제일 멋진 옷차림 뽐내 봐.

He is my boss's **right-hand man**.
그 사람 우리 상사 오른팔이야.

We're through here.
우린 끝났어.

You can **fix my problem**.
너라면 내 문제 해결할 수 있어.

Pick up the forms on the way home.
집에 가는 길에 양식 좀 가져와.

Let me **propose a toast** to my friend!
친구를 위하여 건배.

He is **in his twenties**.
그 사람은 20대야.

Let's **face** the reality.
현실을 직시합시다.

We are not **spring chickens**.
우리는 애송이가 아닙니다.

Come off smoking.
담배 끊으세요.

He's **got a point**.
그 사람 감 잡았어.

Listen up, please.

잘 들으세요.

Get out of the way.

저리 비켜주세요.

Stay up until two o'clock a.m.

새벽 2시까지 버텼다.

I'm getting all **funned out**.

재미 없네.

Nobody is that **heartless**.

그렇게 매정한 사람은 없어.

You're going to **wind up** all alone.

너 나중에 외톨이가 될 거야.

He **built a fire**.

불 좀 지펴줘.

Let's **back to work**.

하던 일 계속합시다.

Everyboy **heads-up**!

여러분들 예고합니다.

Toodles.

안녕

You **proved me wrong**.

당신을 보니 내가 잘못 생각했어.

Dialogue

1. Once Upon a Time

KUZCO Will you take a look at that? Pretty **pathetic**, huh? Well, you'll never believe this, but that llama you're looking at was once a human being. And not just any human being. That guy was an emperor, a rich, powerful ball of charisma.

KUZCO This is his story. Well, actually, my story. That's right, I'm that llama.The name is Kuzco. Emperor Kuzco. I was the world's nicest guy and **they ruined my life** for no reason! Oh, is that hard to believe? Look, I tell you what, you go back a way, you know, before I was a llama, and this will all make sense.

2. Kusco Despot

KUZCO Boom, baby!

RANDOM GUY Your Highness! It's time for you to choose your bride! All right! **Trot out** the ladies! Let's take a look-see. Hate your hair. Not likely·········And let me guess you have a great personality. Is this really the best you could do?

……

KUZCO What is he babbling about? He's like the thing that wouldn't shut up! Anyway, still wondering about that llama in the opening? Well, let me show you the people responsible for ruining my life.

3. Pacha

PACHA Ah, excuse me. I'm here to see Emperor Kuzco. You see, **I got this summons.**

GUARD Inside, up the stairs, and to the left. Just follow the signs.

PACHA Oh, great, thank a lot.

KUZCO Uh, and don't be fooled by the folky, peasant look.

……

KUZCO	You see what I mean! This guy's trouble. But as bad as he is, he is nothing compared to what's coming up next.

4. Yzma

KUZCO	Okay, gang. Check out this piece of work. This is Yzma, the Emperor's advisor. Living proof that dinosaurs once roamed the earth. And let's not forget Yzma's **right-hand man**. Every decade or so she gets a new one. This year's model is called Kronk.
	……
YZMA	It is no concern of mine whether your family has — what was it again? peasant, um, food?
YZMA	Ha! You really should have thought of that before you became peasants! **We're through here**. Take him away. Next!
	……
YZMA	But Your Highness. I was only dealing with meaningless peasant matters.
KUZCO	Whoa. Look at these wrinkles. What is holding woman together? What the.. How long that has been there?
	……
KUZCO	Oh, great. Send him in. Oh, and by the way, you're fired.
YZMA	Fired? What do you mean, fired?

5. Kuzcotopia

KUZCO	Pacha! That's right, you are just the man I wanted to see!
PACHA	I am?
KUZCO	Word on the street is you can fix my problem. **You can fix my problem**, can't you?
PACHA	Sure, I'll do what I can.
KUZCO	Good, good. That's just what I wanted to hear.
	……
KUZCO	Well, that settles it.
PACHA	Really?
KUZCO	Yup, problem solved, thanks for coming.

PACHA That's it? That's all you wanted me for?

……

PACHA Uh-uh-uh-uh- I don't understand how this could happen.

KUZCO Well, let me clear it up for you. At my birthday celebration tomorrow, I give the word, and your town will be destroyed to make way for this! So if I were you, I'd **pickup some change-of-address forms** on the way home.

6. Yzma's Revenge

YZMA He can't get rid of me that easily! Who does that ungrateful little worm think he is? Does he — a little to the left — he has any idea of who he's dealing with? How could he do this to me? Why, I practically raised him!

……

YZMA Of course the real Kuzco! Don't you see? It's perfect! With him out of the way and no heir to the throne, I'll take over and rule the empire! Brilliant!

……

YZMA Ah, how shall I do it? Oh, I know. I'll turn him into a flea. Harmless little flea. And then I'll put that flea in a box, and I'll put that box inside another box, and then I'll mail that box to myself, and when it arrives—ahaahhahaha!—I'll smash it with a hammer.

……

YZMA So, is everything ready for tonight?

KRONK Oh, yeah. I thought we'd start off with soup and a light salad, and then, see how we feel after that.

……

YZMA Excellent! Few drops in his drink, then I'll propose a toast, and he'll be dead before dessert!

KRONK Which is a real shame, because it's gonna be delicious.

……

KUZCO So… **no hard feelings about being let go**?

YZMA None whatsoever. Kronk, get the Emperor a drink.

KRONK Drink. Right. Your Highness.

KUZCO Is something burning?

……

KUZCO He's what, **in his late twenties**?

YZMA	I'm not sure.
KRONK	Saved 'em!
KUZCO	Oh, that's great, good job, very good job.
KRONK	Watch it. They're still hot.
	……
KUZCO	Because you're··· you know. Let's face it, you're no spring chicken, and I mean that in the best possible way.
YZMA	What? A llama? He's supposed to be dead!
KUZCO	Yeah.Weird

Music Break

You Raise Me Up

When I am down and oh my soul so weary
When troubles come and my heart burdened be
Then I am still and wait here in the silence
Until you come and sit awhile with me

You raise me up so I can stand on mountains
You raise me up to walk on stormy seas
I am strong when I am on your shoulders
You raise me up to more than I can be

You raise me up so I can stand on mountains
You raise me up to walk on stormy seas
I am strong when I am on your shoulders
You raise me up to more than I can be

You raise me up so I can stand on mountains
You raise me up to walk on stormy seas
I am strong when I am on your shoulders
You raise me up to more than I can be
You raise me up to more than I can be

❊ Review

He looks really **pathetic**.
그 사람 정말 처량하게 보이네.

The villain **ruined** my life.
그 원수가 내 인생을 망쳐 놓았어.

She **trotted out** her best dress.
어디 멋진 옷차림으로 뽐 좀 내봐!

He is my director's **right-hand man**.
그 사람 우리 상사 오른팔이야.

We're through here.
자 여기게 끝냅시다.

You can **fix my problem**.
당신이면 내 문제 해결할 수 있어.

Pick up the forms on the way home
집에 오는 길에 양식 좀 가져다 줘.

Let me **propose a toast** to my friend!
우리 친구에게 건배합시다.

Have no **hard feelings** about being let go.
내보낸다고 서운하게 생각하지 마세요.

He is in **his twenties**.
그 사람 20대야.

Let's **face the reality**.
현실을 직시합시다.

We are not **spring chickens**.
우리는 애송이가 아닙니다.

❊ Activity 4-1

I Try it on in English.

1. 이건 말도 안돼.

2. 어디 한번 봅시다.

3. 확인해 보세요.

4. 더 이상 할 얘기가 없습니다.

5. 유감이군!

6. 그 사람은 30대 초반이다.

7. 너는 더 이상 애송이가 아니다.

II. Answer the given questions and develop your idea.

1. Who are, among the characters of the movie, responsible for turning Kuzco from a human Emperor to llama? And for what reasons did they betray the Emperor instead of staying as loyal subjects?

2. What is Pacha's personality like?

III. Words to Live by

1. It's better to give than to receive.

2. Haste makes waste.

3. There are two side to every question.

4. The grass is always greener on the other side of the fence.

Dialogue

7. Kuzco LLama

KUZCO Guess where I am right now! Uh-huh, in the bag. Still think I'm not the victim here? Watch, it gets better. Oh, he's doing his own theme music? Big, dumb, and tone-deaf. I am so glad I was unconscious for all of this.

KRONK Mission accomplished.

……

SHOULDER DEVIL Don'tlisten to that guy! He's trying to lead you down the path of righteousness. I'm gonna lead you down the path that rocks.

ANGEL Oh, **come off it**.

DEVIL You come off it!

……

DEVIL **Listen up**, big guy, I've got three good reasons why you should just walk away. Number One: look at the guy! He's got that sissy stringly music thing.

ANGEL We've been through this. It's harp, and you know it.

DEVIL Oh, right, that's a harp, and that's a dress.

ANGEL Robe!

DEVIL Reason Number Two: Look what I can do.

KRONK Wha — what does that have to do with anything.

ANGEL No, no, **he' got a point**.

8. Pacha is Home

TIPO Mom, Mom! I think I'm still growing! Measure me again!

CHICHA Ha! All right.Tipo. Stand still and let's see.

……

CHICHA Look how much you've grown!

DAUGHTER What? Tipo, **get out of the way**. It's my turn again. Measure me. Tipo, Dad's home!

……

DAUGHTER	That's not as impressive as my loose teeth. See?
CHICHA	Okay, Okay, you two. Our deal was that you could stay awake until Daddy came home. Now say good night.
KIDS	Dad, do we have to?
PACHA	No, you two can stay up.

……

CHICHA	So what did the emperor want?
PACHA	Ahem, you know what? He couldn't see me.
CHICHA	Couldn't see you? Why not?

……

PACHA	Sweetie, sweetie, think of the baby.
CHICHA	Pacha, I'm fine. This baby's not coming for a while, but even if it was, I'd give that guy a piece of my mind. That kind of behavior just-just-Uhh! I gotta go wash something. Pacha? You OK?

……

KUZCO	Uh, hehheh. Hi. Excuse me. Two seconds here. Um. I'm the one in the cart. Remember? This story's about me, not him. Okay. You got it? All right.We're gonna move ahead. Sorry to slow you down. Hehhehheh.

9. Kuzco in Pacha's Home

PACHA	Okay, demon llama. Just take it easy. I mean you no harm.
KUZCO	What are you talking about-oh, wait. You're that whiny peasant.

……

KUZCO	I'm an ugly, stinky llama.
PACHA	Wait, OK, your majesty.
KUZCO	Llama face!
PACHA	Shh! what happened?
KUZCO	I'm trying to figure that out, Ok? Ohh-ho! I can't remember. I can't remember anything. Wait a minute. I remember you. I remember telling you that I was building my pool where your house where your house was and then **you got mad at me**. Oh! And you turned me into a llama.
PACHA	What! No, I did not.
KUZCO	Yes, and then you kidnapped me.

……

KUZCO	Hmmm. You're right. That's giving you way too much credit. OK. I have to get back to the palace. Yzma's got that "secret lab." I'll just snap my fingers and order her to change me back. Hey you. No time to waste. Let' s go. Hey, Tiny, I want to get out of this body. Wouldn't you? Now, let's go.
PACHA	Build your summer home somewhere else.
KUZCO	You want to run that by me again?

10. Persistent Kuzco

KUZCO	Scary jungle. Right. Oh, a leaf. Oh. It might attack me. Oh, it's a scary tree. I'm afraid. Ha ha. Please. Never find my way? I'm the emperor, and as such. **I'm born with an innate sense of direction**. OK. Where am I? Wha..
	……
KUZCOOK	That was the freakiest thing I've ever seen. Ah! Hmm. What do you mean?
	……
KUZCO	Hit the road, Bucky. Aah! Ow!

❊ Review

Come off it!
그 일에서 손떼.

He's **got a point**.
그 사람 감 잡았어.

Listen up, please.
잘 들어.

Get out of the way.
저리 비켜.

Stay up until midnight.
자정까지 버텨라.

I mean you no harm.
당신에게 해칠 생각 없소.

Take it easy.
천천히 하세요.

I **got mad at** him.
그에게 화를 냈어.

I am born with **an innate sense of** direction.
나는 타고난 길눈이 있는가 봐.

Hit the road.
길을 떠나다.

❊ Activity 4-2

I.Try it on in English.

1. 좋아지고 있다.

2. 임무 완료.

3. 저리 비켜!

4. 새벽 2시까지 깨어 있었다.

5. 아이는 당분간 나오지 않을 거야.

6. 내게 화내지 마세요.

7. 시간이 아깝다.

II. Answer the given questions and develop your idea.

1. What does Kuzco think of himself as a llama?

2. What does Kronk think about Kuzco?

III. Words to Live by

1. Look before you leap.

2. Every man is mad on some point.

3. The apple never falls far from the tree.

4. Rob Peter to pay Paul.

Dialogue

11. Odyssey to Palace

KUZCO Maybe I'm just new to this whole rescuing thing, but this is, to me, I might be considered kind of a step backwards, wouldn't you say?

PACHA No, no, no. It's — it's OK. This — this is all right. We can figure this out.

……

KUZCO Yaah! Aah! Ow! Whoohoohoo! Aah! Ow! Ow! Uhh! I don't know about you, but **I'm getting all funned out**. Uh-oh.

KUZCO Don't tell me. We're about to go over a huge waterfall.

PACHA Yep.

KUZCO Sharp rocks at the bottom?

PACHA Most likely?

KUZCO Bring it on. Boo-yah! Whoo.

……

KUZCO But now that you're here, you will take me back to the palace. I'll have Yzma change me back, and then I'll start construction on Kuzcotopia. Oh, yeah.

PACHA OK. Now, look, I think we got off on the wrong foot here.

……

PACHA Well, yeah. Nobody's that **heartless**.

KUZCO Mmmm. Now take me back.

……

PACHA You know what? Someday, you're going to **wind up** all alone, and you'll have no one to blame but yourself.

KUZCO Thanks for that. I'll log that way. Now, for the final time, I order you to take me back to the palace.

……

KUZCO Because unless you change your mind, I'm not taking you back. Me, me, me. Moo, moo, moo, huh? What? I didn't do anything. I didn't somebody's throwing stuff. You going to **build a fire** and what? What's going on?

12. Kuzco, Still Alive!

KRONK	He never had a chance.
YZMA	For all eternity. Well, he ain't getting any deader. **Back to work**. Kronk, darling. I must admit **you had me worried** when you mixed up those poisons, but now that Kuzco is dead, all is forgiven.
KRONK	Ah. Oh, yeah. He's···dead, all right. Hehheh. I mean, you can't get much deader than he is right now. Unless, of course, we killed him again.
	……
KRONK	I just thought I'd give you **the heads-up** in case Kuzco ever came back.
YZMA	He can come back!
KRONK	Yeah. That would be kind of awkward — especially after lovely eulogy.
YZMA	You think? You and I are going out to find him. **If he talks, we are through**! Now let's move.

13. Omen

TIPO	Dad, look out.
CHICHA	Tipo, what is it?
TIPO	I had a dream that Dad was tied to a log and **was careening out of control** down a raging river of death!
CHICHA	All right, all right, it's OK.
TIPO	It was awful!
CHICHA	Shh! It's OK, It's OK. Tipo, calm down. It was just a dream. Your dad's fine. He just went back to see the emperor.

14. Believe it or Not···

PACHA	I thought you were a changed man.
KUZCO	Oh, come on, I had to say something to get you to take me back to the city.
PACHA	So all of it was a lie?
KUZCO	Well yeah. No, wait, Yeah, yeah, it was all a lie. **Toodles**.
	……
PACHA	Why did I **risk my life** for a selfish brat like you? I was always taught

	that there was good in everyone, but, oh, **you proved me wrong**.
KUZCO	Oh, boo-hoo. Now, I feel really bad. Bad llama.
PACHA	I could've let you die out there in that jungle, and then all my problems would be over.
KUZCO	Well, that makes you ugly and stupid.

……

KUZCO	What are we gonna do? Aah! What are we gonna do? We're gonna die! That's it for me!
PACHA	No, we' not. Clam down. I have an idea. Give me your arm. Okay, now the other one. When I say go, push against my back, and we'll walk up the hill. Ready? Go.

……

PACHA	Working on it. OK. Here's the deal. Stretch out your neck and I'll grab the rope.
KUZCO	How do I know you won't let me fall after you grab the rope?

……

PACHA	Almost. Got it! It's stuck.
KUZCO	Take your time. No hurry here.

❊ Review

I'm getting all **funned out**.

재미 없는 걸.

Nobody is that **heartless**.

세상에 그토록 매정한 사람은 없다.

You're going to **wind up** all alone.

결국 외톨이가 되고 만다.

He **built a fire**.

불을 지폈다.

If he talks, **we are through**.

말만 하면 우리는 끝장이야.

Let's **back to work**.

자 하던 일 계속합시다.

Everyboy **head-ups**!

여러분 모두 조심하세요.

You **had me worried**.

너 걱정 된다.

The boat was **careening out of control**.

배가 걷잡을 수 없을 정도로 기울어진다.

Toodles.

안녕.

You **proved me wrong**.

너를 보니 내 생각이 잘못 되었다.

❊ Actvity 4-3

I. Try it on in English.

1. 한번 도전해 보렴.

2. 당신은 결국 혼자 남고 말 거야.

3. 불 좀 피워라.

4. 하던 일 합시다.

5. 당신에게 경고를 한 적이 있는데.

6. 조심하세요!

7. 진심일 때 나에게 고백하세요.

II. Answer the given questions and develop your idea.

1. Who are most concerned about the job given to Pacha?

2. What did Pacha find concerning Kuzco on the way to the palace?

III. Words to Live by

1. Too many cooks spoil the broth.

2. Might makes right.

3. The bread always falls buttered side down.

4. Old soldiers never die, they just fade away.

Dialogue

15. One-Time Thing

PACHA You just saved my life…that there is some good in you after all. I think there is. Hey, you couldn't let me fall.

KUZCO Come on, **what's big deal**? Nobody's that heartless. **Don't read too much into it. It was a one-time thing**.

PACHA Right. Sure. Well, we better get going. With that bridge out, it's a four-day walk to the palace.

……

KUZCO Well, yeah, but I hope you realize that doesn't change a thing. I still building Kuzcotopia when I get back.

PACHA Well, four days is a long time. **Who knows**? Maybe you'll change your mind.

16. Searching Kuzco's Whereabouts

KRONK Yeah. Tell me about it. No, no, it's not you. She's not the easiest person to get close to. There's a wall there. Trust me.

YZMA Are talking to the squirrel?

KRONK I was a junior chipmunk. I had to **be versed in** all the woodland creatures. Please continue.

……

KRONK Hey, it doesn't always have to be about you. This poor little guy has had it rough. Seems a talking llama gave him a hard time the other day.

……

KRONK I hate being in the middle. Squeakly, uh…squeak, squeaker, squeaking: Jaguars? No kidding? Brutal. Uh, **could you give us a little room here**? A little bit more, please.

17. Welcome to Mudka's Meat Hut

PACHA	Where are you going?
KUZCO	I'm just going up to slip into the kitchen and have a word with the chef.
PACHA	You're gonna get us thrown out.
KUZCO	Please. With this disguise, I'm invisible.

……

YZMA	We've been walking around in circles for who knows how long. That is the last time we take directions from a squirrel. I should have done away with Kuzco myself when I had the chance.
KRONK	Oh. You really gotta stop beating yourself up about that. Uh-oh. I'll get you another one there, Yzma.you are using that fork there, pal? Hey, don' t I know you?

……

KUZCO	Look, all I know is the food looks iffy. All right? And I'm not the only one that thinks that, I'm sure.
KUZCO	So, I'm just checking to make sure you're going to take the main course up a notch.
YZMA	Is there anything on this menu that isn't swimming in gravy?
KRONK	Hang on. I'll go ask the chef.
KUZCO	It's a simple question. Is there or is there not anything edible···on this menu?...I didn't ask him about dissert yet?

……

YZMA	What's taking so long?
KRONK	Pickup!
YZMA	Kronk! What are you doing?
KRONK	Kinda busy here.
YZMA	Why am I not surprised?
KRONK	Your order's up!
YZMA	Ohh! Oh, well, while you're at it, make me the special. And hold the gravy!

……

KRONK	Cheddar spuds coming up.
KUZCO	Spuds yes, cheese no.
KRONK	Hold the cheese.

YZMA	No, I want the cheese.
KUZCO	Cheese me no "likeee".
KRONK	Cheese out.
YZMA	Cheese in!
KRONK	Cheese on, **make up your mind**!
KUZCO	Okay, okay, on second thought….
KUZCO AND YZMA	Make my potatoes a salad.

18. Kuzco the Dupe

PACHA	Look, there's two people in there looking for you.
KUZCO	What?
PACHA	A big guy and a skinny old woman.
KUZCO	Wait. Was this woman scary beyond all reason?
	……
KUZCO	I get it! You don't want to take me back to the palace. You want to keep me stranded out here forever
PACHA	No!
KUZCO	**This has all been an act**, and **I almost fell for it**.
	……
YZMA	Oh, this entire mess is your fault.
KRONK	What'd I do?
YZMA	If you hadn't mixed up those poisons, Kuzco would be dead now! There'll be no more diversions until we track that llama down and kill him!
KRONK	Said I was sorry. **Can't we just let it go**? Not even on your birthday.
YZMA	Kuzco must be eliminated. The empire will finally be rid of that useless slug.
KRONK	You've got a point. Nobody really seems to care that he's gone, do they?

19. Miss the Wanted

KRONK	That peasant at the diner! He didn't pay his check. He's the peasant who

I saw leaving the city who disappeared into the crowd with Kuzco on the back of his cart. He must have taken him back to his village, so if we find the village, we find him, we find him, and if we find him, we find Kuzco. Oh, yeah, it's all coming together. Yzma!

……

PACHA And just as it started to go, he grabbed me before I fell. So there we were standing on the cliff, and the ground started to rumble·········He's a lousy llama.

I mean, a really lousy llama·········. Okay, we're just going to stop at the house and get some supplies.

KUZCO Then we'll be on our way, right?

20. Ransacking the House

CHICHA So, remind me again how you're related to Pacha?

YZMA Why, I'm his **third cousin's** brother's wife's step-niece's great-aunt. Hehheh.**Twice removed**.

……

CHICHA You know, I am sorry that you had to come all this way, but as I said to you before, you may recall, Pacha is not here. I'll be sure and tell him you came by.

YZMA Oh, would you, please? That would be just great. Oops. Silly me.

……

CHICHA Go I'll stall them long enough for you two **get a head start**.

PACHA Thanks, honey.

KUZCO You have a lovely wife. They're both very pretty.

……

CHICHA What do you mean **the door is stuck**? Try jingling the handle.

YZMA There is no handle in here.

CHICHA There's not? Are you sure?

YZMA All right. I've had enough of this. Tell us where the talking llama is, and we'll **burn your house to the ground**.

21. Fighting over the Vial

KRONK Well, **you got me. By all accounts**, it doesn't make sense.

YZMA Oh, well, **back to business**.

KUZCO Okay, I admit it. Maybe I wasn't as nice as I should have been, but, Yzma, do you really want to kill me?

……

KUZCO I can't believe this is happening!

YZMA Then I bet you weren't expecting this!

……

YZMA Ha ha! Finish them off!

DEVIL Hey, you're not backing down now, are you, big guy?

KRONK Uh, here's the other guy? You!

ANGEL Sorry I'm late. Some, what'd I miss?

……

ANGEL Now, now, remembers guys. From above, the wicked shall receive their just reward.

KRONK, ANGEL AND DEVIL That'll work.

KRONK Strange. That usually works

22. Back to a Human

COW Hey. I've been turned into a cow. Can I go home?

YZMA You've excused. Anyone else?

……

KUZCO Yeah! We're flying! Uh-oh! We're not getting anywhere with you picking the vials. I'm picking the next one!

PACHA Fine by me!

KUZCO Give me that one! Don't you say a word.Aah!

……

SOLDIER For the last time, we did not order a giant trampoline.

TRAMPOLINE MAN You know, pal, you could have told me that before I set it up.

……

PACHA Got it!

KUZCO **What are the odds** of that trap door leading me out here?

……

PACHA Here, uh, let me get this for you.

KUZCO Well, see you on the other side.

OLD SUBJECT	You stop **being so hard on yourself**. All is forgiven.
KUZCO	You're sure?
OLD SUBJECT	It's not the first time I was tossed out a window, and it won't be the last.

❊ Review

What's the **big deal**?

큰일 났습니까?

Don't **read too much into it**.

거기에 큰 의미 부여하지 마세요.

It was **a one-time thing**.

이번 한 번 만입니다.

Who knows?

알게 뭐람?

She **is versed in** songwriting.

그 여자는 작곡에 능하지.

Could you **give us a little room** here?

잠깐 자리 좀 비켜 주시겠습니까?

The food looks **iffy**.

음식이 뭔가 수상해.

On **second thought,** I decide on it.

다시 생각해 보고 그 것으로 결정했어.

This **all has been an act**.

이 모든 것은 연극이었어.

I almost **fell for it**.

거기에 속아넘어갈 뻔 했지.

Can't we just **let it go**?

그냥 내 버려 둘 수 없었나?

We had **a head start**.

우리가 먼저 시작했다.

On your mark! **Get set**! Go!

출발선에! 준비! 출발!

The door **is stuck**.

문이 안 열린다.

The second cousin in the second **remove.**

2대 손위(손아래) 6촌

By all accounts, it doesn't make sense.

어느 모로 보나 그것은 말이 안 된다.

Let's back to business.

자 하던 일을 계속합시다.

Stop being so hard on yourself.

자신을 나무라지 마세요.

What are **the odds** of winning?

우승 확률이 얼마나 됩니까?

❊ Activity 4-4

I. Try it on in English.

1. 뭐가 대단해?

2. 내가 떨어지도록 내버려 둘 수 있었잖아!

3. 그렇게 무정한 사람은 없어.

4. 그 사람은 가까이 하기게 쉬운 사람이 아니야.

5. 저는 고추장은 빼 주세요.

6. 다시 생각해 보니 이것이 낫다.

7. 잠깐만요.

II. Answer the given questions and develop your idea.

1. What was Kuzco like before he was retransformed into a man?

2. To whom does “two people in there looking for Kuzco” refer?

III. Words to Live by

1. Need makes the old wife trot.

2. A good neighbor is better than a brother off.

3. Mighty oaks from little acorns grow.

4. Many a true word is spoken in jest.

Music Break

Movie Titanic: My Heart Will Go On

Every night in my dreams
I see you, I feel you
That is how I know you go on

Far across the distance
And spaces between us
You have come to show you go on

Near, far, wherever you are
I believe that the heart does go on
Once more you open the door
And you're here in my heart
And my heart will go on and on

Love can touch us one time
And last for a lifetime
And never let go till we're gone

Love was when I loved you
One true time I hold to
In my life we'll always go on

Near, far, wherever you are
I believe that the heart does go on
Once more you open the door
And you're here in my heart
And my heart will go on and on

You're here, there's nothing I fear
And I know that my heart will go on
We'll stay forever this way
You are safe in my heart
And my heart will go on and on

Worksheet

Taking Dictation Practice in Lyrics

✽ Lyrics Dictation Worksheet 1

Musical Cats : Memory

Midnight,
not a sound from the ___________.
Has the moon lost her memory?
She is smiling alone.
In the lamplight,
the___________ leaves collect at my feet,
and the wind begins to __________.

Memory,
All alone in the moonlight,
I can dream of the old days.
Life was beautiful then.
I remember the time
I knew what __________ was.
Let the memory live again.

Every street lamp seems to __________
a fatalistic warning.
Someone __________,
and the street lamp gutters
and soon it will be morning.

Daylight,

I must wait for the sunrise,

I must think of a new life

and I musn't________.

When the _________comes,

tonight will be a memory too

and a new day will begin.

Burnt out ends of smoky days,

the________ cold smell of morning.

The street lamp dies,

another night is over,

another day is dawning.

Touch me,

it's so easy to _________ me,

all alone with my memory

of my days in the sun.

If you touch me, you'll understand

________ __________ ________.

Look, a new day has begun

❀ Lyrics Dictation Worksheet 2

Solveig's Song

The winter may pass and the spring disappear

The spring disappear

The summer too will _________

and then the year

And then the year

But this I know for certain: you'll come back again

You'll come back again

And ________ _____ ________ you'll find me waiting then

You'll find me waiting then

Oh-oh-oh ....

God help you when wand'ring your way all alone

Your way all alone

God grant to you his _________

as you'll kneel at his throne

As you'll kneel at his throne

If you are in heaven now _______ _______ _______

In heaven for me

And we shall meet again love and never ________ be

And never parted be!

Oh-oh-oh ....

❀ Lyrics Dictation Worksheet 3

The Beatles : Let It Be

When I find myself in times of trouble
Mother Mary comes to me
Speaking words of wisdom
Let it be
And in my hour of __________
She is standing right in front of me
__________ ________ _____ ________
Let it be

Let it be, let it be
Let it be, let it be
Whisper words of wisdom
Let it be

And when the broken hearted people
Living in the world _________
There will be an answer
Let it be

For though they may be _________ there is
Still a chance that they will see
There will be an answer
Let it be

Let it be, let it be
Let it be, let it be
There will be an answer

Let it be

Let it be, let it be

Let it be, let it be

Whisper words of wisdom

Let it be

Let it be, let it be

Let it be, let it be

Whisper words of wisdom

Let it be

And when the _________ ______ ________

There is still a light that shines on me

Shine until tomorrow

Let it be

I wake up to the _______ _____ _______

Mother Mary comes to me

Speaking words of wisdom

Let it be

Let it be, let it be

Let it be, let it be

There will be an answer

Let it be

Let it be, let it be

Let it be, let it be

Whisper words of wisdom

Let it be

✽ Lyrics Dictation Worksheet 4

Simon and Garfunkle : Bridge Over Troubled Water

(Don't trouble the water)

I won't

(Give it up)

(Why don't you, why don't you, let it be?)

Um hum

(Still water ______ _______, yes it do)

I know that

(Whoa yeah)

Yeah, if you only believe

(Don't trouble the water)

Said I wouldn't

(Give it up)

(Why don't you, why don't you, let it be?)

Umm

(_______ ________ run deep)

Yes it do

(Yes it do whoa oh ho yeah)

If you only believe

When you're down now

When you're on the street

When ________ ________

Somehow I will comfort you

I'll ______ _____ _______

Whoa when darkness comes

And your love around

Just like a bridge over troubled water

I will lay me down

(Like a bridge)

Just like a bridge

(Over troubled)

Over troubled water I will lay me down

Sail on silver moon

Sail on by

______ _____ _____ ______ _____ ______

All of your dreams are on their way

(See how they shine?)

Ooh and if you ever ______ ____ _______

(Need a friend)

Look around and _______ ______

Just like a bridge over troubled water

I'll be there to lay me down

(Like a bridge)

Like a bridge over

(Troubled water)

Troubled water I will lay me down

Ooh, ______ ____ ______ ________.

Yes I will

(Don't trouble the water)

Said I wouldn't

(Give it up)

❖ Lyrics Dictation Worksheet 5

Movie Avatar : I See You

I see you

I see you

Walking through a dream I see you

My light in darkness __________ hope of new life

Now I live through you and you through me

____

I pray in my heart that this dream never ends

I see me through your eyes

Living through life ________ ________

Your life shines the way into paradise

So I offer my life as a _________

I live through your love

You teach me how to see

All that's beautiful

My senses touch your word I never pictured

Now I give my hope to you

I ___________

I pray in my heart that this world never ends

I see me through your eyes
Living through life flying high
Your love shines the way into __________

So I offer my life
I offer my love, for you

When my heart was never open
(and my spirit never free)
To the world that you have shown me
But my eyes could not ___________
All the colours of love and of life ever more
Evermore

(I see me through your eyes)
I see me through your eyes
(Living through life flying high)
Flying high
Your love _________ the way into paradise
So I offer my life as a sacrifice
And live through your love
And live through your life

I see you
I see you

✽ Lyrics Dictation Worksheet 6

You Raise Me Up

When I am down and oh my soul so _________
When troubles come and my heart __________ be
Then I am still and wait here _____ ______ __________
Until you come and sit __________ with me

You raise me up so I can stand on mountains
You raise me up to walk on __________ seas
I am strong when I am on your shoulders
You raise me up to more than I can be

You raise me up so I can stand on mountains
You raise me up to walk on _________ seas
I am strong when I am on your shoulders
You raise me up to more than I can be

You raise me up so I can stand on mountains
You raise me up to walk on __________ seas
I am strong when I am on your shoulders
You raise me up to more than I can be
You raise me up to more than I can be

✽ Lyrics Dictation Worksheet 7

Movie Titanic: My Heart Will Go On

Every night in my dreams
I see you,
I feel you
That is how I know you go on

Far across the __________
And _________ between us
You have come to show you go on

Near, far, wherever you are
I believe that the heart does go on
Once more you ________ _____ _______
And you're here in my heart
And my heart will go on and on

Love can touch us one time
And ________ for a lifetime
And never let go till we're gone

Love was when I loved you
One true time I _______ _____
In my life we'll always go on

Near, far, wherever you are
I believe that the heart does go on
Once more you open the door
And ______ _______ in my heart
And my heart will go on and on

You're here, there's nothing I ________
And I know that my heart will go on
We'll stay forever this way
_______ ______ _______ in my heart
And my heart will go on and on

저 자

이봉형

서울대학교 영어영문학과 학사, 석사, 박사
Cornell University
University of Massachusetts-Amherst
Indiana University-Bloomington 방문연구원
현재 대전대학교 영어영문학과 교수

저 · 역서

최적성이론의 이해 (한신문화사, 2000, 공저)
영어학강의 (한국문화사, 2001, 공저)
영어학의 최근논점 (한국문화사, 2005, 공저)
최적성이론 해보기: 이론과 실제 (한국문화사, 2009, 공역)
Snap Shots of Heroes of Our Mind (신아사, 2010)
Selected Top Epoch-Making Speeches (신아사, 2010)
차용어 음운론 (한국문화사, 2013)

Screen Enlglish

First Published March 2013
SHINASA Publishing Co.
28-36 NokBeon-Dong, EunPyung-Gu, Seoul, Korea
Registered: 9-52 (Jan. 5 1956)
Tel: 02-382-6411
Fax: 02-382-6401
E-mail: shinasa@chol.com / Homepage: www.shinasa.co.kr

ISBN: 978-89-8396-788-6

Printed and bounded in Korea

₩ 10,000